Courage at Work

Courage can shape our lives, as well as the workplace and business outcomes. Willingness and ability to take risks make space for major decisions. And it's more than something to admire in others: courage can be learned, and this book will teach you.

Building on examples from a 30-year international career in marketing, coaching, and political activism, Florence Guesnet introduces the pioneering concept of the "courage zone." This shifts courage from unattainable heroism to a competence that can be built with five steps: recognize fear, perceive your heart's desires, analyze reality, make a decision, and take the step. The book begins by strengthening the reader's courage as an individual, inspiring a bold mindset and vision, and including hands-on exercises. The book then goes on to show readers how to carry their courage into organizations and inspire others, addressing questions of governance, strategy, and everyday team encouragement against the backdrop of 21st century demands and typical paralyzing fears.

Current and aspiring leaders in small, medium to large organizations will be empowered to take risks, surmount obstacles, and grab opportunities with this book's effective tools to build courage in themselves and their teams.

Florence Marie Guesnet is a graduate economist author, executive coach, and marketing executive with an international career at companies like Procter & Gamble, Estée Lauder Companies, and Heineken International. In her work, she empowers individuals and teams to go for ambitious goals, effective strategies, and courageous action. Florence is German-French, mother of three adult children, married, and lives in Cologne, Germany.

"Courage at work - Taking on challenges from today's world, growing as a leader, instilling trust in others - all this requires courageous leadership. Packed with personal authentic stories, this instructive and practical book is an essential and wonderful read if you want to empower courage."

Ann Francke *Chief Executive, Chartered Management Institute, Order of the British Empire*

"Inventing new taste experiences, creating a new advertising campaign, innovating how we work - impossible without courage. Courage at Work from Florence Guesnet inspires and empowers to step into unchartered new terrain".

Bram Westenrbink *Chief Commercial Officer, Heineken International*

Courage at Work

Your Path to Strong Leadership

Florence Marie Guesnet

Routledge
Taylor & Francis Group
NEW YORK AND LONDON

Designed cover image: Shutterstock

First published 2025
by Routledge
605 Third Avenue, New York, NY 10158

and by Routledge
4 Park Square, Milton Park, Abingdon, Oxon, OX14 4RN

Routledge is an imprint of the Taylor & Francis Group, an informa business

First published in German ("Mutig weiter! Dein Weg zu guter Arbeit und starker Führung") by Books on Demand, Norderstedt, in 2022

ISBN: 9781032949925 (hbk)
ISBN: 9781032949918 (pbk)
ISBN: 9781003582724 (ebk)

DOI: 10.4324/9781003582724

Typeset in Sabon
by codeMantra

Contents

Acknowledgments

I am grateful to many friends, experts, and trailblazers who have inspired, contributed, and encouraged me to write and finish this book. To name a few in person:

Benno Dorer, former Chief Executive Officer of Clorox, for an in-depth interview on ethics and morals, difficult moments, and the power of encouragement.

Ann Francke, CEO of the Chartered Management Institute and OBE, for her unwavering passion for inclusive leadership, and her ability to bring about enlightening conversations.

Oliver Kastalio, former CEO and Chairman WMF, for the intensive exchange on courageous leadership.

Dr. Markus Klimmer, Chairman of the Board of Directors at HH2E, consultant, policy advisor, for giving me access to his amazing network, for sharing his courage crucibles with me, and for his passion for justice.

Dr. Angelika Schrand, Managing Director of Contur GmbH, for her insights on innovation, change management, and respectful leadership.

Marc Nicolaudius, Managing Director of the Magnetec Group, for his enthusiasm and encouragement for leadership that makes change really happen.

Francine De Bruyckere-Geerts, friend and business partner, for the joint development of encouraging concepts, training, and coaching.

Oscar for his mastery of language, his calm attitude, and the good-humored, yet tough challenges of his mom's view of the world.

Oliver for his precision, wisdom, and constant presence and support in my life. Thank you for this and for much, much more.

Chapter 1

Introduction

Here it is: the moment you feel resistance, fears, and risks, and yet you gather your strength, make the decision, and take the leap. Even though the outcome is unknown, you are determined to take a risk and get active. Because you want to stand up for your values, satisfy your curiosity, or pursue an ambition. That is courage.

I have always said about myself: "I am the most courageous fearful person I know." I am highly alert to risks and undesirable outcomes. The words "dangerous," "I'm afraid" or "watch out" ring out in my head and from my mouth quite often. Regardless, people around me have often called me brave and encouraged me to offer strength and inspiration to others. So, they can let go of fear when in doubt and take brave action instead. I traveled daring paths as a young person in politics and later as a manager in international companies. Those paths and my talents have not made me the German Chancellor, CEO, or national heroine — but a successful manager, a sought-after coach, and a happy mother and wife with three children. One with many experiences and decisions that can be instructive for other people in similar contexts — and which I have written down for you, dear reader, in this book.

I meet a lot of people who have "lost their courage" — who walk the tightrope of being surrounded by constraints, jealous colleagues, or opportunistic superiors. These people are mentally exhausted and frustrated. Unfortunately, this is the prevailing culture in many organizations – no one likes to say anything authentic anymore, as it comes off as unwanted criticism and rattling delicate foundations. The results are organizations that operate at the lowest common denominator, with mediocre results and feeble employees. Organizations in which managers will be heard saying: "I have to pick my battles," which, in other words, means they actually see many conflicts but only have the capacity or resources to find constructive solutions for a few of them. With this book, I seek to address this lack of willpower to confront, to wrestle with what the right path is. I want to mobilize your courage to leave the familiar behind. I already do this in

DOI: 10.4324/9781003582724-1

coaching sessions, workshops, and training courses – and hopefully, also with this book.

Many of the examples and stories in this book relate to my personal experiences in companies – either as a leader in a corporation or as a consultant and coach. Therefore, this book may be more accessible and relevant for people who work in medium and large companies and aspire to or already have influence there. However, the concepts and strategies described in this book are also transferable to many other areas of life, enabling you to recognize and trace the courageous path in your family and social life.

My core concern with this book is that our world, our fellow human beings, and we as individuals need courage for the future. I would like to offer thoughts and ideas that will make the ride there easier. So that you don't have to look back on countless missed opportunities. So, we don't constantly tell ourselves: "I should have said that earlier," and we as a society are not confronted with the timid bravehearted being overrun by a swarm of aggressive scaredy-cats. Whether it's personal happiness, professional and business success, or saving the world: it doesn't work without courage.

Editorial Note

All the stories that I share here have happened but, of course, can only reflect my perception of them. Many names (people and companies) have been changed to protect people's personal rights and then marked with an asterisk.

Part 1

Individual Courage

Chapter 2

Courage Fundamentals

Courage is the capacity to overcome fear, even if the consequences might be unpleasant, painful, or difficult to calculate. You experience courage in this fascinating moment when you feel the inner resistance, the fear, the uncertainty – often as a knot in your stomach – and then, perhaps trembling inside, you spring into action. Your heart is pounding in your throat, adrenaline is rushing through your body, you are still aware of the fear, but you have relegated it to the back of your mind. And you act. That is courage. You need it when you raise your voice in a group you don't know when you contradict someone more powerful – or when you don't know whether you're biting into a hot or a mild chili.

What is fascinating about courage is that it does not require the absence of fear, but rather that fear is a prerequisite of courage. Courage enables me to perceive fear and then choose to overcome it. To act in pursuit of a goal, a value, a principle that is important to me. That is courage. Courage is therefore also very individual: it is your ability to perceive your personal hesitation, your individual fear, your worries and to then take the risk and make the necessary effort.

Courage is different for each of us. I have met people who have spent millions of euros on an advertising campaign without batting an eye but didn't dare to ever contradict their boss. There is the "physically courageous" person who likes to take risks when skiing, mountain biking, or in a boxing match, and about whom onlookers might say "I would never dare to do that." But the same person can also be very awkward socially and afraid to raise their voice in front of a large group.

That's why I say, no one is always courageous, everywhere. And what appears to us as courage, for them is perhaps the most mundane, even boring routine. Your courage leads you out of the cage of your personal fears, and you can mobilize, train, and strengthen it. I cordially invite you to do so with this book.

DOI: 10.4324/9781003582724-3

Courage Shapes Our Life

For many years, I have been working intensively on the subject "courage." I am driven by the question of what role "courage" plays in societal, organizational, and personal progress. I am convinced that courageous action plays a key role, and thus I have been trying to find out how we can strengthen our courage. To do so, I don't carry out empirical primary research but rather conduct interviews, read guidebooks and scientific explanations, and draw courage-boosting methods from my training courses. In my conversations, I find out what other people view as "courage," how managers use it, and how they promote it. CEOs, self-employed people, politicians, and I are frequently impressed by how courage shapes our lives, how it creates great opportunities, and how it gets us on track for a fulfilled life. Whether it's an "I like you" to your high school crush, an "I'll do it now" when applying for a CEO role, or becoming a mother – without courage, these wonderful, fulfilling, and life-changing events would not have happened.

One of my most formative moments of courage had a massive impact on my career.

As usual, we all rolled our eyes as soon as Alan* left the room. "This micro-management is driving me crazy," says Rick*, the Finance Director. "How can you dish out so much and ask so little questions?" Catherine* asks, still flustered. And so on and so forth. Alan is the managing director of our business unit, and we are the global management team of a billion-euro business. He is a brilliant leader: strategic, strong-willed, with a nose for opportunities and risks and with a lot of operational depth and endless energy. The latter tended to drive us mad or into a certain frustration and underperformance, as we didn't feel like he fully trusted us. At the same time, Alan was a brilliant boss for me: unselfish, committed, and demanding.

Although Alan was my dream boss, I decided to accept an offer from another company and quit: out of professional curiosity, homesickness (we had been living abroad for many years), and because we wanted a more stable environment for our children again. So, my strong-willed boss invited me to dinner at the fanciest restaurant in town. When I got into the car, he simply said: "Tonight, I'm going to convince you not to quit." I replied: "Tonight, you'll understand that I'm quitting." A few hours later, I had achieved my goal, but he hadn't achieved his. Suddenly Alan asked: "Now that that's settled, I'm interested in your feedback. How do you see my work, me as a manager and what I could do better?" I started with all his positive qualities, which was easy and quite comfortable for both of us. When I was done with those, I gathered all my courage. All I could think about was how much better Alan could be if he knew his blind spots. And surely nothing could really go wrong, as I would be quitting anyway. So, I offered him my perspective, a mirror to his weak behavior with various examples. He kept looking at me in disbelief and saying: "I can't believe I'm doing this. That's completely unacceptable." In the end, he was just amazed that I was the first person to offer him this mirror – and thanked me multiple times for my openness and courage.

My great admiration for Alan grew even more that evening – I hadn't expected such dignity and self-criticism. And what happened next? Well, I resigned and, according to my colleagues, Alan had already made efforts to improve. But I was gone. Years later, my office phone rang. "Yes, hello, this is Lisha Noreen*. Our new CEO, Alan Wayne, has asked me to find you. For an assignment in our European headquarters. Would you be willing to talk to me?" Yes, I was! My current job had completely exhausted itself and me, and my hunger for a new learning curve was huge. In Alan's company, I became Vice President for my area of expertise in Europe and was able to take on a key role in the European management team. My tailwind for making a big difference in that company was the words from Alan when we talked about my joining his company: "I will always trust you." My courage had made me trustworthy. You can build on trust.

Courage Can Be Learned

Courage is the capacity to overcome fear, even if this can have unpleasant, painful, or unpredictable consequences. In my understanding, courageous behavior can be learned, it is not a character trait.

The key to acting with courage in your life is wanting to learn courageous behavior. What happens when you learn? Putting it simply, you create new connections in your brain and with your body that lead to new knowledge, new skills, and new attitudes. And the more you build up and use these new connections, the better and more confidently you can use the new knowledge, accomplish something new, behave differently, and approach life with a fresh attitude. This is how motivational researcher Dr. Michaela Brohm-Badry sums it up: "Courage can be learned by having positive experiences. Our brain learns when we successfully overcome a challenge or have positive experiences with people and surround ourselves with good things. These experiences are the key." (Lutteroth, 2022) (translation by the author)

Courageous behavior becomes easier and easier through many little tests of courage: if you familiarize yourself with the risk and learn this new way of acting, you will generally feel less fear, for which you would then have to gather your courage to overcome it. That's why people who take particularly high risks constantly practice, drill, and repeat. Whether in military, health, or security-related professions: in simulations actions are rehearsed so that in the actual moment of crisis, the situation feels familiar, routines can be used, and people can act without fear. The next chapter, "The Courage Zone - From Fear to Action," is where you will learn the steps you can take to mobilize your courage. You can strengthen your courage in the long term by:

- Being self-aware and having a clear idea of what you want (and don't want) in your life
- Recognizing fear and not "pushing it away"
- Learning to realistically assess mistakes and risks
- Appreciating your path to acting courageously
- Practicing actions that that are difficult/scary for you
- Asking people to support you in your journey

But why would you want to learn courage? Sometimes the thing you really, really want will be outside your comfort zone. Off to new shores!

Courage – What for?

You mobilize courage for three main reasons:

1 Courage for yourself: You have personal goals and aspirations for yourself and have the courage to tackle them (e.g., an athletic goal, a stay abroad, your next educational qualification or just flirting with Kim). Your "desires" for shaping your life give you the strength to be courageous
2 Courage for "it": You have a project that you believe in and want to see realized. The "pull" of this idea motivates you to find courage
3 Courage for others: You have clear ideas about how life in your environment, in our society, should be shaped – and how it should not be. Your primary motivation is the social, political, and societal responsibility you feel

These motivations can mix and overlap and are not necessarily distinguishable from one another. The founder of a start-up for a ground-breaking healing method may install very progressive ideas for employee retention, while simultaneously dreaming of a multi-million payout on the stock market.

I point out these three motivations because they are all legitimate and necessary forms of courage, but each of us develops them to different degrees. This distinction can help you understand which form of courage comes easily to you and where you might want to practice more courage in the future.

Courage-Maker: Curiosity

"Between courage, cockiness, and breakneck behavior" (translated by author) is a heading in an article by Schmitt (2018) about scientific self-experimentation. Driven by scientific curiosity, people have had bulls charge toward them, drunk a cocktail of gastritis-causing bacteria, infected themselves with yellow fever, or had a rubber tube smeared in olive oil pushed from the brachial vein to the heart. The last of which led to the invention of the heart catheter in 1929. These are just a few gruesome examples of where curiosity can lead: these breakthroughs happen beyond the comfort zone!

Curiosity moves us into the growth zone and we satisfy our curiosity through courageous action. We learn new things, try what is unfamiliar, and discover the unknown. Becoming a mother was a huge curiosity project for me: what happens during pregnancy, what is childbirth like, what kind of person is coming into the world, and what might happen next? What does motherly love feel like, and how does it develop? So endlessly exciting, surprising, difficult, and beautiful. It's the biggest adventure of my life that just goes on and on.

In my work, I am also driven by curiosity. I have left companies because everything was too familiar and well-known for me. Five years after I had turned my back on Procter & Gamble, I had a wonderfully melancholic dinner with my most important colleagues – and the topics of conversation were the same as half a decade earlier. That's when I knew I had made the right move.

What are your curiosities for which you want to mobilize your courage?

> Courageous action shapes your life, *with courage you can set the course*. Courage is not a character trait you are born with. You can *consciously activate courageous action* and the motivation for this can be a *personal goal*, a *project* that is important to you or a *responsibility* that you want to fulfill. In addition, pure curiosity, the "want-to-know" is often encouragement enough.

References

Lutteroth, J. (2022). Chef oder Grizzly. Spiegel Wissen, 1/2022, 89.

Schmitt, S. (2018, July 15). Wissenschaftliche Selbstversuche: Der Beweis bin ich. *Zeit Online*. https://www.zeit.de/2018/29/wissenschaftliche-selbstversuche-geschichte

Chapter 3

The Courage Crocodiles

As much as we can build, practice, and strengthen courage, it is also vulnerable. There are circumstances that weaken our courage. Everyone can imagine that in times of political oppression, for example, people are less likely to articulate their political opinions – the risk is perceived as too great. And many of us have already experienced how a tyrannical boss can stifle an open exchange of ideas.

In my search for feeding courage, I came across powerful killers of courage – the "courage crocodiles." You may check in with yourself – which have you come across in your life, and how did they affect you?

1 You feel isolated and lonely. Distrust, belittlement, and even humiliation dominate. When you don't connect with others, you are less courageous. There is a lack of trusting conversation with which you can gain a deeper understanding of the situation and weigh your options for action. There is a lack of appreciation, a lack of being seen, and this undermines your courage. A lack of connection also means less support and encouragement from others
2 Your inner compass goes haywire. Health, personal, or professional crises, and massive, persistent negative stress can mess you up. What is important to you, what do you need, when do you feel well? If you don't have these answers, it's difficult to mobilize your courage – it needs your direction and clarity
3 The situation is confusing. Conflicting demands and goals, changing strategies in your environment, your own experience, and what others say don't fit together at all: it's too difficult to understand the "terrain" for you to take steps of courage
4 Reinforced concrete environment. Whether at work or in your private life – if you are only surrounded by people who feel good when nothing changes, and might even react aggressively to change, courage becomes difficult. Your needs for growth and change, and the courage

DOI: 10.4324/9781003582724-4

you muster for this, threaten these people's needs for stability, security, and familiarity

5 People who scare you. These are often people who have a strong tendency toward narcissistic disorder. With these people, "admiration" is the currency of human relationships. That's why there's the nice saying "God forgives, but a narcissist never does."

In the following, I am offering strategies to strengthen your courage against these destructive forces.

When Mistrust and Belittlement Dominate

It was another long day at work. A lot to do, a lot of political games in the multi-national company I was working for, and once again my boss postponed our jour fixe, for which I had been waiting for weeks (or has it been months?). Like a child, I look forward to my evening appointment with a colleague and friend, a relaxed, gossipy get-together (see page 121), where I can get some information on how I'm viewed within the company, a sort of confirmation of my standing. Then her message arrives right before our appointment: "I can't make it today. I have to cancel our appointment." When I get home, it hits me: I'm incredibly sad, I cry, and fear overwhelms me. I feel threatened by the inscrutable power games, by my manipulative boss and jealous colleagues who, in my mind, are spinning strange intrigues. My friend's cancellation hurts me to the core. Later, I call Oliver, my husband. We have a good conversation, and I can calm down a bit. And this episode shows me that I need to take more care of myself and, above all, spend more time with people I trust and with whom I feel connected.

Isolation, rejection, and humiliation are anxiety-inducing for every one of us. The human need for trust, acceptance, and belonging is universal and drives our behavior.

A feeling of constant belittlement is extremely stressful – social acceptance is a basic human need, an "instinctual goal" (Bauer, 2013, p. 35) and consequently, its violation has far-reaching effects. Neurologists have now discovered that our brain perceives social exclusion, rejection, contempt, and humiliation as similar to physical pain (see Bauer, 2013). Such experiences are anxiety-inducing, can paralyze you, or even make you aggressive. You want to defend yourself, perhaps fight back, and often start to mirror or copy the ostracizing behavior. A tit for tat, an eye for an eye. I recognize that I've had this fighting reflex time and again. Sometimes I have given in, and hopefully more often, I was able to take a step back. Taking a step back meant creating a little "space" of consideration, checking in with my principles and values, and wondering about the dynamics I would be fueling. And choosing a path that was consistent with my values and bringing about the person I want to be.

In coaching, the experience of isolation and distance is a frequent topic raised by coachees. Dismissive superiors, diverging objectives within an organization, a few egotistical people – and you're already in a fine mess. How do you put these courage crocodiles on a diet?

1 You're not feeding them self-doubt. If exclusion hurts you, there's nothing wrong with you. Your need for connection, recognition, openness, and kindness is totally okay. You are a human being with human needs
2 You create connections and friendships. You actively approach people, find common ground, are friendly, and look to connect. If you can't do this at work because years of bad leadership have allowed mistrust, intrigue, and egoism to flourish, then you do it outside the workplace
3 See if you can take on more and more responsibility and lead in such a way that discouraging behavior has increasingly less power and influence. We discuss how you can make an organization more courageous in the second part of the book

A Wayward Inner Compass

When your inner compass goes haywire, the path out of fear becomes difficult. However, as soon as you realize this, you have already taken the first step toward finding courage. How can you re-mobilize your inner compass?

My first question is always: are you getting enough sleep? Second question: when was the last time you had a proper break, at least two days, and when was the last time you had more than a week to rest, switch off, and wind down? If the amount of sleep and rest you get has been insufficient for a long time, your strength is sapped, and, consequently, so is your courage. Mobilize everything you can to get enough sleep and take breaks again and again. Your inner compass may get back on track with enough sleep and breaks.

Look at the "Camp Future" to find orientation for the future (see Chapter 5). Perhaps you need closure from a stressful episode before you can muster the strength for something new – "Acceptance, Forgiveness, and Self-love" is the chapter for you (see Chapter 5).

Confusing Context

Evidently, the amenity for confusion is clarity. Collecting the facts, assessing the situation with others, asking questions – all this can help you to explore the terrain and find the stepping stones for your path toward courage. Find allies to help you get your bearings. Sort through the information and thoughts you have so that you can gain confidence and overcome your fear.

There can be moments in which you are acutely unable to create clarity. That is "chaos." The first few weeks (or months) of a pandemic. Floods in your region. A cyber-attack on your company.

In chaotic situations, you act "on sight." You want to be aware that, in this great confusion, you don't know much, can only react acutely and no big steps are possible until the situation has cleared up. In a chaotic situation, courage – stepping out of your comfort zone and moving into the learning zone – is not always your first choice. As everything around you is in motion and changing at top speed, sometimes waiting or "driving with foresight" is the better option. The flow of information is poor, and you don't even know what your options are. Rushed, "big" decisions can fall on your toes.

Stagnant Surroundings

Changing hurts, growing hurts. Being stuck where you don't belong can be unbearable. If you have ended up in a situation where you don't feel in the right place and your impulses to bring about change are repeatedly rejected, then take good care of yourself – and maintain your respect for others. You may make considerate offers (see Chapter 7) and don't take other's reactions personally.

If you want or need to stay in that challenging context, be prepared for a long journey of patience, at the end of which you may be successful.

Whether at work or in your private life, if you are mainly surrounded by people who only feel good when nothing changes and even react aggressively to any semblance of change, courage becomes difficult. Because courage offers growth and change, people will slow you down.

People Who Trigger Fear

It's our first coaching session. Ms. Ganem* describes her situation at work. She is proud of her promotion a year and a half ago. She has worked long and hard for this step and is responsible for setting up a sales organization that is to add many millions in sales to the company. But now, numerous problems have arrived with her new role, and she is looking for new ways of doing things. She is hesitant about what she can and wants to tell me. As we talk, her trust in me grows, and she becomes more and more shaken as she tells me about her boss. Tears begin to flow: "He's yelling. He shouted at me. I've never experienced anything like it. Never! And it happens time and again." Ms. Ganem is afraid of her boss because he yells at her (and not only at her, but that's another story) and accuses her of mistakes and bad work. We discuss how his shouting and her fear affect her. There have been sleepless nights. During a phone call with him, she hung up because he was shouting again. She says, "I should never have done that," instead of, "He should never have yelled at me like that, so I hung up because I won't put up with his behavior."

She is altering her entire behavior so that she gives him as little reason as possible to start yelling at her once more. She thinks about what she can, may, should, and must say. Internally, all her focus is on managing her boss' behavior. With incredible discipline and willpower, she somehow manages to fulfill her actual work tasks. She is exhausted, frustrated, and discouraged.

What is important when we deal with people who (want to) intimidate and manipulate us?

As already described, these are often people who have a strong tendency toward narcissistic personality disorder. As long as you admire them, flatter them, and dance to their tune, everything is "okay." Narcissistic people always want to come out on top, want others to be dependent on them, and relate everything that happens around them to themselves.

You will not change these people. Whatever their history and motives are, all you can control is your behavior toward them. Your goal must be not to "feed" the narcissist(s) with your feelings. They live off your fears and insecurities.

The answer you can give again and again when this person attacks you:

If that's how you see it.
If that's your view.

And that's it. No further justification, explanation, or debate. You don't share your feelings, wishes, and burdens with these people. They would only use them for the next manipulative step anyway. If you don't provide them with ammo for the next blow, they may just lose interest in talking to you. And you will have managed your energy well since you didn't reveal anything about yourself by saying: "If that's how you see it."

Those Courage Crocodiles!

There are circumstances and people that act as *courage crocodiles*. If you feel *isolated*, find yourself in a very *confusing situation*, or *lack inner clarity*, then every step can feel arduous. You might also find yourself in *a state of paralysis* if you are surrounded by people who don't want to change anything and/or are even actively manipulating or threatening you. Perhaps your courage is being "eaten away" by such circumstances.

Surround yourself with people who feed your courage. *Recognizing your own needs* and taking them seriously, distinguishing between what you *can and cannot change in the short term,* and separating yourself from *personal encroachments* – all of this can strengthen your courage.

Reference

Bauer, J. (2013). *Schmerzgrenze: Vom Ursprung alltäglicher und globaler Gewalt.* Karl Blessing Verlag.

Chapter 4

The Courage Zone – From Fear to Action

In training courses and experiential education, we learn about the concept of the comfort, growth, and panic zones.

We feel safe in our comfort zone, everything is familiar and often repeated, and we know our way around. Driving, cooking our favorite dish, going shopping. Here, we feel relaxed.

As soon as we leave what is familiar, we move into the growth zone – sometimes also called the learning or stretch zone. This is where we acquire new skills, try out new approaches and experiment. Depending on the difficulty, complexity, and intensity of this way of learning, it works – or we end up in the panic zone, in which we don't learn anything because we are overwhelmed and can't absorb anything. It's like taking your first driving lesson on Monday morning in Paris on Place Charles de Gaulle instead of in the Cash & Carry parking lot after closing time.

This model is illustrative. And yet – for me, it falls short. To get out of your comfort zone, you often need to make a conscious effort on your own. That's why I offer a fourth zone: the courage zone. This lies between the comfort zone and the growth zone, which comes a little later. Because you don't make really difficult decisions in a single step. Your courage enables you to get out of the comfort zone and into the growth zone. "Be brave!" is easier said than done. Before you enter the growth zone, you need the courage to leave the comfort zone definitively – which is a process in itself, one that sometimes only takes a few seconds or minutes but can also take weeks or months for some big decisions. That's about the importance of the new "courage zone."

In the courage zone, your gut, heart, and brain have a lot to say. There is a multifaceted inner negotiation taking place and you are the lead negotiator (Figure 4.1).

Step One: Curiosity of Fear

The first step into the courage zone is being curious about your own fears. Your gut is telling you more or less directly: I'm scared! At this point, you

DOI: 10.4324/9781003582724-5

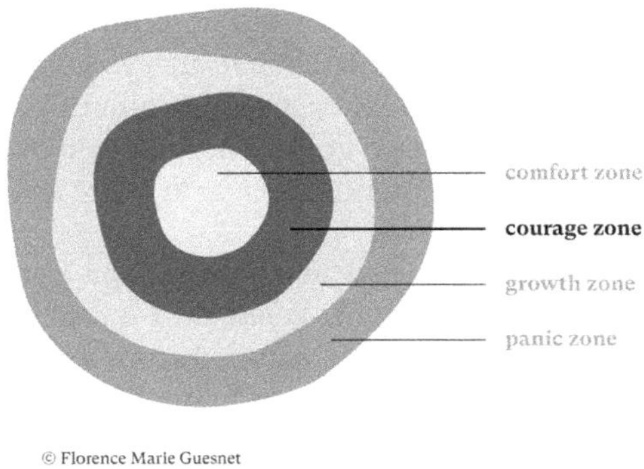

Figure 4.1 The courage zone lies between the comfort and growth zone.
Source: the author.

can simply give in and stay in your comfort zone. Or you can curiously ask your gut what kind of fear it is, thereby shifting it from a physical, instinctive signal to a conscious and controlled consideration. Listen to your gut, but don't yield to it. Feel the fear and then bring it from instinct into reflective contemplation. One of the bravest, strongest, and most important people of the 20th century put this idea in a nutshell:

> I learned that courage was not the absence of fear, but the triumph over it. The brave man is not he who does not feel afraid, [...] but he who conquers that fear.
>
> Nelson Mandela

Perceive, observe, and understand the uncertainty and hesitation. What happens? Threats trigger an instinctive reaction in our brains. Hormones are released, and everything is on alert. The problem is that in this instinctive reaction, our brain does not differentiate between a real-life threat (encountering a bear in the woods) and other emotionally taxing triggers (an angry boss or a nasty remark from a colleague). Scientists measure the same reaction to "harmless" stress factors as to "actually dangerous" threats. When fear rules, the amygdala runs the show and uses all our brain energy. Our conscious and reflective thought center is acutely undersupplied because our body "thinks" the situation is a matter of survival. That's why it's so important to transfer the instinctive fear into conscious observation and thus overcome the unconscious, spontaneous reaction. Unless there's an actual bear in your path.

In the non-bear-related moment of fear, there may not be energy for this "fear-curiosity." Then you need to find the energy later, look at the situation again, and explore what exactly triggered your fear in the first place.

To explore your fear, this is an exercise you can follow: place both hands on your stomach. Feel your emotions. What images emerge? What do you hear? What does your body do when you reevaluate the fear – listen to your heartbeat, do you feel hot or cold, where does tension arise in your body? Perceive all of this and remain curious. You are not the fear – fear is there and wants to be understood.

Be sure to differentiate between fears caused by external events and those that you create all by yourself. What do I mean by that? Concerns about climate change, the coronavirus pandemic, or even the difficult business situation in your company can trigger fears. What will the future look like, what can I do, is my family safe, is the company perhaps going into restructuring? You are worried, and the following steps in the courage zone can get you to take action.

The worries you make for yourself are your own judgments, fantasies, and stories you tell yourself about the world and your place in it. Worrying is like praying for what you don't want. In building my business, I am constantly working against the fear of being seen as a supplicant, an annoying salesperson, or even a loser who must chase after customers instead of giving out numbers on a waiting list.

A constant stream of LinkedIn posts, newsletters, or anecdotes from more successful colleagues then feed this story, that really good consultants "never had to do acquisition" and that I'm probably not really good. I am aware of this fear, it is part of my story. But it doesn't help me in the future. That's why I'm working with myself and my coach to overcome this persistent idea of being seen as a failure. I replace this inner image with a more life-serving one. Inner fears invite you to overcome them and build inner freedom.

> Fear knocked. Trust opened the door. No one was outside.
>
> From the Chinese cultural area, source unknown

Step Two: Cross Your Heart!

With an understanding of your fear, take the next step and question your heart. Continue to be honest with yourself and go into reflection:

- What is really important to me?
- What am I curious about?
- What do I wish for?
- What needs to change?

"Courage comes from commitment." You talk to your heart about what gets you out of your comfort zone. Place both hands on your heart, feel, and listen to what it has to say about your longing. Perhaps it is talking to you about a value that you cannot (or can no longer) live up to in your comfort zone. Or about a wish that you want to fulfill, an irresistible curiosity. Feel how big this intention is within you, and whether it can surpass your fear. You can capture this intention in your thoughts, though even better in conversations, written down, or painted in a picture.

This clarification – whether it's with yourself, a trusted person, or a coach – can be surprisingly plain and simple. Eva suddenly knows that she doesn't want a second child. Abdul knows that he doesn't want to be self-employed at all, since he likes the clarity his current position offers. Crossing her heart, Olivia can only talk about the fact that she wants to write a book and will subordinate everything else in the pursuit of this goal.

Strengthen Self-Awareness and Confidence

Without values, principles, goals, and convictions – a clear understanding of the "self" – courage becomes very difficult. It is your awareness of the "self" that gives you the strength to take risks. If you don't care about anything, you don't need courage. Instead, you let yourself be pushed around and see what happens. That's one option. The other option is to become aware of your dreams and desires and to "talk it out" with others. And soon you will find the courage to take a stand and find opportunities. If you find it difficult to perceive your own wishes and needs, then you are: not alone! Many people grow up with "having to," "being told to," "not being allowed to," and have trouble finding and articulating their own desires and ambitions. Create space for this and find out – alone, with a confidant, or a good coach. You can also use the "Camp Future" for this.

What Is Important to You, How Do You Want to Live?

How do you imagine your life? What do you do, with whom? What do you want to achieve in a certain time frame, what opportunities do you want to create and use? What is particularly important to you in your private life, how do you envision your professional life? What are you curious about?

The answers to these questions can guide you in big and small decisions. And the more conclusively you know the answers, the faster your heart will know whether fear ought to be overcome. Courage comes from commitment.

You can also write down your answers in a personal manifesto. At regular intervals, you can look at how they manifest themselves in your life and how things can or should continue. Likewise, what works well and what is difficult. Where you might have "failed" and where you would now like to direct your energy.

The Values that Guide You

In a seminar on self-management with a group of students, "values" are on the agenda. In small groups, they talk about their individual choices from a long list of words capturing values like "freedom," "justice," "respect," "loyalty" and the like. When I ask them to come back to the plenary session, they all ask for more time. Even after the extension, they are reluctant to return – the discussions were so important, profound, and exciting. Everyone sensed that, like a compass for life, values guide their choices and actions.

Being aware of your values, you understand much better why you may find some situations or decisions so stressful and difficult. You sense that your values are "at risk" and this can be very unsettling. Courage is about acknowledging this reality and deciding how to proceed and taking responsibility when doing so.

Which values are essential for you? Look at what gives you energy, resolve, and joy – most likely this has something to do with your values. When checking in with your fear, what values empower you to overcome that fear?

Sometimes, fear tells you that core values of yours have been hurt. If you defend a wrongly accused co-worker, this serves your value of "justice" and "honesty" – yet your value of "belonging" and "security" might be at risk. Becoming aware of your values is very important for courage. If values are in jeopardy, for most of us this means "crisis" – you cannot live up to your values. Solving such a dilemma is outside of the comfort zone, and thus, it needs courage. Unfortunately, I don't know the source of one of the best quotes I ever heard while listening to the radio at night: "The story begins when no option fits your values!"

"Cross your heart," the second step in the courage zone, can therefore mean a lot of inner conversation. That's completely okay – and the more these inner clarifications, the easier your answers will come to you. Now you have taken the second step – your convictions are telling you that you want to leave your fear behind? And the opportunities and risks are still a little too opaque for you to decide?

Getting a grasp of the risks and opportunities, understanding critical facts and information is the next step in the courage zone. This step will allow you to weigh your heart's desire against the odds of success.

Step Three: Perceive Reality!

When making important decisions (taking up or dropping out of university, changing jobs, buying a house, going abroad...) with long-term consequences, you'll want to carry out a thorough analysis to gather as much information as possible for your decision and then decide how to proceed.

Use all your sensors and your mind: which key facts are available and need validation, which scenarios are likely? What do you foresee, do you have an intuition, are there weak signals for a big opportunity? Other people might help you to look at reality from various perspectives, adding to your perception:

- People who have already taken similar steps to the one you are contemplating
- People who know you and your situation well
- People who are affected by your decision

Figure out the facts and be as sure as possible that you are not working solely on assumptions. Whether it's about admission requirements for a degree program, formal requirements for a job, the HR department's approach to an official complaint – the more you know, the smarter you can be in selecting your approach. And check what risks you really want to take. Part of perceiving reality is anticipating others' reactions to your courage.

When you play through possible reactions, don't let yourself be guided by wishful thinking but play through the entire spectrum of positive and negative reactions. Especially from people who are greatly affected by your actions. You want to be prepared for the vehemence of the reaction and guard yourself emotionally and factually.

Evaluating Situations: Small Scenario Technique

It would be impossible to try and count how many times in my professional life I've heard the phrase "He is going to kill me if I...." To this day, I cringe when someone says something to that effect. I find this notion horrible, and I believe the image to be inappropriate for any professional situation. Unless you're working for a terrorist organization or the Cosa Nostra, this sentence is a massive self-deception and leads you to a state of emotional panic. No need to go there. Pick the risk apart – what your boss threatens to do, they might not put into practice. And whatever they do may have a much smaller effect on your life than you feared initially. As I, and others, said before, worrying is like praying for what you don't want.

Before you let yourself be discouraged by the worst possible outcome: Here is a little help for realistic assessment. If this is too mechanical for you, you can skip this digression. If you enjoy picking things apart, you can use this template (Figure 4.2):

The last question is very important, it helps you to understand the result the outcome has for you: How do you interpret certain effects for yourself? This is an instructive way to be honest with yourself. It is what the courage

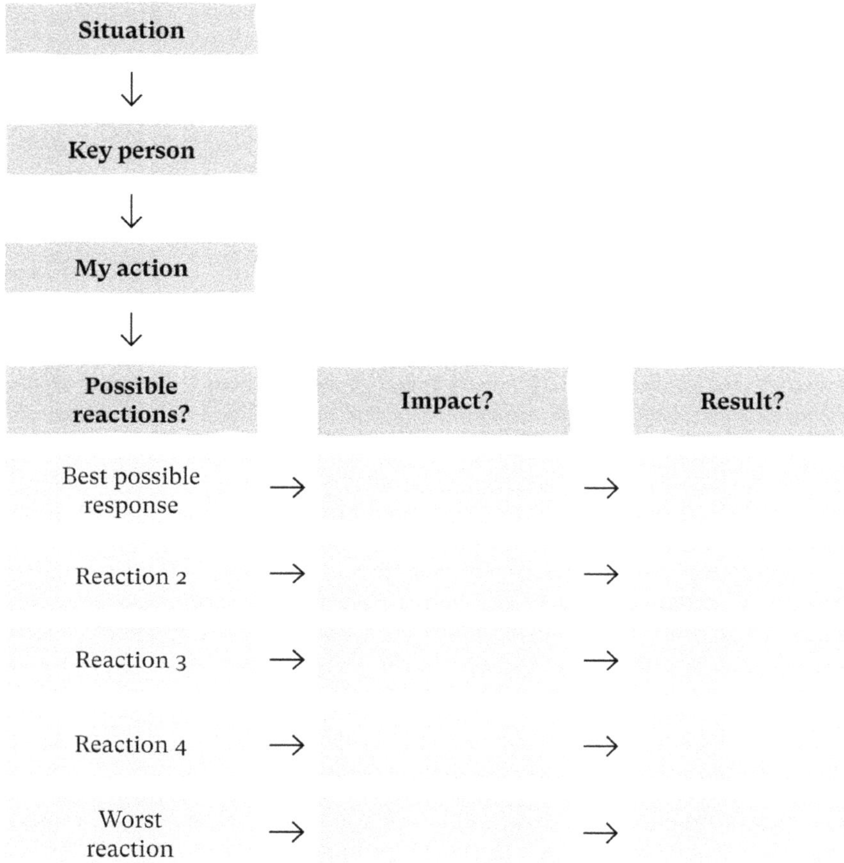

Figure 4.2 Template for scenario of options and outcomes.

Source: the author.

scenario looked like for me after I left an interview that had already been typed up for final approval lying around for four (!) months (Figure 4.3):

In my mind, there are five possible reactions to my late request: one is ideal, two bring extra work, and the last two are truly annoying. So, let's look at the next scenario: not asking for approval. I have a 100% chance of being annoyed – the interview will not be authorized or published.

My conclusion:

1 Whether it's already too late and the interviewee is angry anyway because it took so long – my chance to find out is to send over the interview and hope that he doesn't care and is just glad to hear from me again

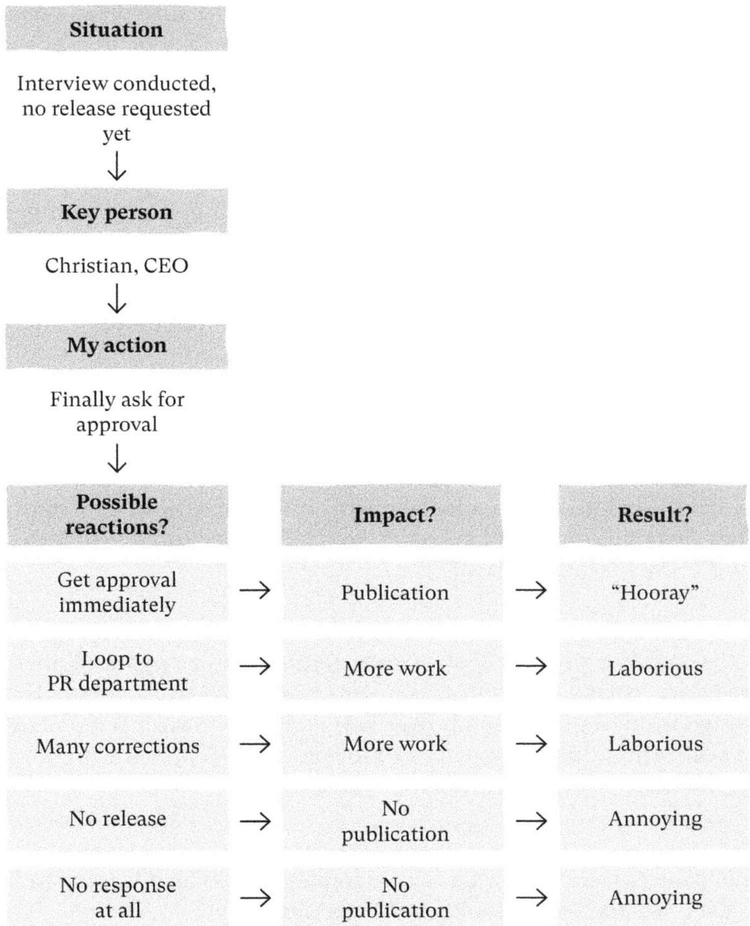

© Florence Marie Guesnet

Figure 4.3 Florence's scenario "ask for approval – or not."

Source: the author.

2 If I don't do anything or if he doesn't respond, I'll get annoyed. And then the interview won't be published. The same result as doing nothing. So, it's better to act, if there is no worse outcome in sight
3 I may have to put in more work than I'd like to and it gets published. So, here we go

And with the "So what?" options, I was able to look at my vanity (What, I don't get an answer?) and my unwillingness to worry about the final details. My dedication to talking to many people about the topic of "courage" eventually got me moving. I sent the interview, promptly received approval and a nice email, all is well. Now I know, that I can save myself the internal back and forth next time.

This "scenario technique" is another tool to help you overcome spontaneous anxiety, engage in conscious reflection, and thus leave your comfort zone.

Step Four: The Decision

Ultimately, from the concoction of mind, gut, and heart, you will decide if you want to overcome your fear and take the path of courage. You trace your three steps:

How big is your fear, what story does it tell you about the world and about yourself? Is it clever and protecting you? Or is it stupid, following old patterns and making you feel smaller than you are?

What does your heart tell you about your desires, your priorities, your curiosities? What gives you a lot of energy and makes your eyes light up?

What facts, insights, and considerations did your mind give you? Can you find a smart way forward?

> Power, properly understood, is the ability to achieve purpose. [...] One of the greatest problems of history is that the concepts of love and power are usually contrasted as polar opposites. Love is identified with a resignation of power and power with a denial of love. What is needed is a realization that power without love is reckless and abusive and that love without power is sentimental and anemic.
>
> Martin Luther King

What is your power? If courage is overcoming fear, then it is good to know what gives you the strength to act courageously.

We were already in our second video conference with Daniel*. Daniel, the country head of a huge operating unit, was furious with my employee – Anna* – and me. He accused us of misleading him in a decision on a product launch. Anna's interpretation of a preliminary study had promised him that the launch would work, i.e., that it would bring more profitable sales into his coffers. But one year after the launch, the thing was a flop. And that's exactly what we warned about in our summary of the preliminary study. So, why was he so angry with us? Well, he wasn't. He was angry with my boss, who had forced him to introduce the product. He didn't want to confront him directly, so he preferred to take his anger out on the head of market research and weaken her position. And he wanted to find a scapegoat for his poor figures, so the "misleading" done by the head office was a great argument! It should also be said that Daniel was not only the head of a huge national operation but also one of the most influential people at the second management level, with a hot line right to the head of the company.

In this moment, what was my fear and what was my "power" to be courageous? This constellation may not trigger any fears in you, or it may trigger completely different ones than mine:

1 I have made a mistake by allowing the incorrect interpretation of the study to pass
2 My employee feels left alone
3 Daniel attacks my department and we lose credibility
4 I'll make an enemy in Daniel if I don't agree with him

Conclusion: Shit. This is not great. Where can I draw my power from now?

First, I draw strength from my mission at the company. And that is to respect facts – and not opinions – as a basis for decision-making. I want to defend the role of my department because it is the basis of our work. Second, I draw strength from the leadership principle of "creating and protecting trust": Anna's interpretation of the study had my backing a year ago. And so does it now, even when an influential person turns up the pressure. Third, I draw strength from my analytical expertise – I take another look at the study, its key figures, and our interpretation, and make sure that we were arguing in a methodologically sound way. And my fourth strength is my rebelliousness. I don't like to buckle, especially when someone expects me to, because they know that I'm a newcomer in a company who has worse cards than them. No way.

Faced with my fears and my power(s), I got through the conflict. I stood in front of Anna and rejected the blame being put on us. Anna hadn't expected that and started to trust me. Daniel remained angry with me, but I put up with that since, in the long term, I thought that being true to the facts was more important than scratching the backs of powerful people.

You have a lot of power, too. It could be educational qualifications, your favorite person, your network, your rhetoric, your resilience, your empathy – create your personal power list. Be aware of how much power you have and can mobilize at a given moment. You can pull out the list when you are stuck in the zone between analysis and conclusion and want to make sure you know how you have grown so far and what you can use in this new moment. Now you make up your mind and are excited about what is to come.

Step Five: The Magic Moment

That magical moment when you do it. Sign the check, book the ticket, stand up, and say "no." Your heart beats fast due to the immense excitement of overcoming your fear. Simply sublime.

Now you're in the growth zone – your decision is making itself felt in your life, it's manifesting. You can find out which of your fantasies come true and whether they might be completely different from what you thought before.

Not only that – as you step into the growth zone and experience learning and, crucially, success, your comfort zone grows. When you sat behind the wheel for the first time, you perhaps couldn't even imagine driving at more than 40 km/h in the city, not to speak of 120 km/h on the highway. And today? You don't associate these speeds with fear or courage at all, they're in your comfort zone. You can apply this example to all areas of life.

For us personally, for the people around us, and for the projects we are involved in: whenever we seek courage, we are on the path to change and growth. Of course, our courage doesn't always lead us to where we had hoped to go. We didn't come first in a competition, our dream job went to someone else, or we fell flat on our belly after jumping off the 5-meter diving board. Ouch. And in most cases, that's it: we are one (perhaps painful) experience richer and wiser.

> Courage is often a lack of insight, whereas cowardice in many cases is based on good information.
>
> Peter Ustinov

This quote describes the other side of the coin – without proper reflection and understanding of the situation, courage can be naïve. We should walk the path from the comfort zone to the growth zone consciously, reflectively, and with a healthy sense of unpleasant consequences. Dwelling in the comfort zone is not necessarily due to a lack of courage. Rather, it confirms that this zone is comfortable.

Let's enjoy this comfort zone and treat each other to it. I grew up in the Rhineland, and the most beautiful belief on this subject is "Let's be happy for others." This book can support you when staying in your comfort zone is no longer life-serving, when compromises hurt, when missed opportunities lead to bitterness or when infractions erode us.

Crossing the Courage Zone into the Growth Zone

Perceive fear, mobilize your convictions, perceive realities, make up your mind, and then act courageously. This is how courage works. *Courage is not a question of character, but a skill you (learn to) utilize.* You can mobilize courageous action in five steps:

1. *Fear is the starting signal* for inner curiosity: what is this gut feeling telling me, what do I want to do with it?
2. You find your conviction by "*crossing your heart*": you decide what is important to you, what you want to take risks for
3. *Analyze* the situation and *review* the facts, also from different perspectives: the mind looks at opportunities, risks, and facts and develops apt, courageous steps
4. In your decision, you *bring together your stomach (the fear), heart (the conviction), and head (perceiving realities)* and, then, choose your next step

And the *magical moment, it happens* – you jump, you sign, you say what has long needed to be said, and you do what you have long wanted to do.

Chapter 5

Mindset for Courage

Your mindset is your attitude, your approach to life, to yourself, and to others. It is a product of your experiences, successes, and adventures to date. Which country you live in, which (if any) religion shapes your upbringing and life today, and which guiding principles your parents wanted to pass on to you: all influence your mindset.

The crucial thing about mindset: it is not genetic and unwieldy in us, but dynamic and changeable. I would like to offer you the opportunity to use your mindset for life-enhancing courage and show you tools that can help you do this.

Camp Future

As part of step two of the courage zone, I suggested to strengthen your self-awareness and your self-confidence. In Camp Future you can reflect, discover your dreams and desires, and recognize the opportunities you have.

Take your calendar and find at least three hours for a meeting with your future. It's best to have a buffer at the end, maybe the meeting is so exhilarating that you want to stay longer. Prepare the meeting carefully – it's important! Make sure you are undisturbed. If you are a visual person, have pens and paint, sheets of paper, and material for a collage ready. If music is your medium, let music accompany you on your journey.

Now paint your desired future – with words, color, or song. The time frame you choose is up to you – let it be at least one year, better five or even ten years. Start a dialogue with your future, and explore what your desired life would look like. Below are some aspects you might want to consider.

With the questions "What I make possible" and "The world needs me for...," I express that we are not isolated amoebas but part of a whole. The questions are not aimed at your "usefulness" or "productivity" but at the meaning you wish to instill your life with. What is happening in the world, what do people want, and what do you want to be a part of? Use this exercise to find out, express, and feel this for yourself (Figure 5.1).

DOI: 10.4324/9781003582724-6

CAMP FUTURE

My future life in the year: ________ ❶

What I bring about:
Who I am now:
What is important to me:
My relationships with others are...
My material situation is...
In terms of health, I feel...
I am particularly happy about...

What I had the courage to do: ❷

____
____
____
____

What have I left behind? ❸

____
____
____

How was that possible? ❹

The world needs me for...
I really want to:
Important choices I made:
Milestones achieved:
Supporting people:
Resources mobilized:

Figure 5.1 Camp Future template.

Source: the author.

At the end of the three hours, look at your desired future. Is it good? What can you do to make it even better? If you are happy with your vision of the future, enjoy this moment!

You have brought about crucial inner clarifications with your vision. In conversations with others, you can deepen and strengthen your new resolutions, insights, and energy. You can adapt your vision of the future at any time since life is not static. "Things won't stay as they are."

That's why I offer further reflections and help in the following chapters to (re-)activate your courage when things get a bit bumpy and tough, or when you seem to be heading straight into a brick wall.

Courage-Accounting

In my interviews about courage, there is always that "aha" moment when it becomes clear how courage has shaped our lives, enabled important turning points, and opened new paths. With the template for your own "courage-accounting" (Table 5.1), you can discover your own courage path. Use it to account for the important episodes of courage – and even, when courage did not kick in.

Look at the result of your courage bookkeeping. How much do you owe to your courage, when did it ever hurt you, how many opportunities went unused – ones that have you wondering what could have happened? What

Table 5.1 Courage accounting template

I was courageous and I see this positive effect in my life:	I was courageous and I see this negative effect in my life:	I was not courageous, and I still wonder:

do the lists tell you about yourself? And about your future opportunities? What are you planning to do, what do you want to change?

The experiences in the second and third columns harbor a danger: they can create resentment, grudges, and a lot of negative energy. A list of missed opportunities, blame, and even bitterness and shame. That's why I considered leaving this question out. And now it's in there after all, because acceptance, forgiveness, and self-love are also part of living courageously (Table 5.1)

The Courage Crucible: Personal Legends

People love stories. Stories give meaning to what has happened, they move us, and we remember them easily. Similar to beliefs and values, stories can strengthen – or weaken – our courage and vitality. Take a piece of paper and write down all the experiences in which you, in your eyes, showed courage. Make the list as long as possible. This can range from skipping school in seventh grade to confronting an abusive colleague to buying a house – write everything down.

Now go through the list and mark experiences you can describe as "personal legends": events in which you brought about positive change with the help of courage, those that shape your personality today and whose consequences reverberate still. The previously mentioned conversation with Alan* was one such "personal legend" for me, as was the episode at Vassar College. But back to you: which experience stands out? Tell yourself the whole story in as much detail as possible. Maybe tell it to people who are important to you. Write the story down and make it part of your novel of life.

Another tip: keep the list. You can always add episodes that come back to you or new opportunities to test and witness your courage.

Inner Beliefs

"Oh, I don't think he's here anymore. While he was waiting, I already told him that you were going to hire me!" This is Thomas' response when the interviewers in a job interview want to end the intensive and energetic conversation with him because another candidate has arrived and is waiting for his chance to apply for the position of managing director. General laughter ensues, the interview ends, and the other candidate gets their chance. But the job goes to Thomas. Was Thomas courageous? What do you feel when you read about such cheeky, arrogant banter? Well, Thomas didn't say that to his competitor, the company just liked his quick-wittedness and perceived self-confidence. He didn't get the job because of his chutzpah but because of his qualifications. And – his courage was well received and recommended him for the job.

I would never have thought of saying something like that off the top of my head. It would have violated my beliefs and values: don't be aggressive, don't put anyone down, we're all in the same boat, only performance matters – these are the dominant thoughts when I think of "competitors." I would not consciously want to gain an unfair advantage. I'd be ashamed if I behaved that way. I sense inner resistance to get my dream job with quick-witted, cheeky, and maybe even aggressive comments, despite knowing that only one person can get the job. Yet, someone else might choose other actions, following their own convictions and beliefs.

Inner beliefs guide us. Being aware of them can be very helpful for your courage as well as consciously choosing the ones that make you strong(er). And for two very different reasons:

Your beliefs can be courage killers, they can be limiting. In my life, one of the most formative family mantras was something to the effect of "There's no need for that!" – the "killer argument" of my mother and among us siblings when it came to "material frivolities."

I am not talking about the Mercedes convertible or an expensive watch but about the desire for ice cream or buying the latest brand jeans. "There's no need for that!" was the killer argument with which every burning desire had to be extinguished immediately. The mantra was fed by my Protestant-pietist background on my mother's side and the very strained material situation of our family of seven after the untimely death of my father. Even today, the sentence frequently finds itself on the tip of my tongue. I recall it when raising my children, during the early financing of my consulting firm, or earlier when budgeting important projects. But what does this have to do with courage? If I follow this belief, I have too little resources to achieve my goals. I need courage to push this transmitted belief aside in order to achieve my wishes and goals.

With the question "What do you tell yourself about yourself?" I send workshop participants into a round of "expressive writing." If you write for longer than about 20 minutes and don't pay attention to spelling and "right or wrong," the "subconscious" takes over more and more – and your conscious self no longer controls what you write. When the participants come back from this exercise, I ask them to read through their own text. One participant has tears in her eyes as she says: "It's all so negative, nasty, and grim. I'm reading very harsh things about myself." I ask if anyone would ever say these things to another person. Most people shake their heads – they wouldn't speak to others in such harsh and unrelenting ways, deprived of kindness. Many people have self-limiting beliefs that should be reflected upon and, ideally, silenced in situations where being courageous is more important.

Beliefs can also give you strength. "Things will be alright," or paragraph 3 of the Cologne Basic Law, "Et hätt noch immer jot jejange," can bring ease and confidence into your life.

The power of beliefs lies in the fact that they are so internalized that they work unconsciously and are subliminally sending you their "message." The ancient practices of praying, chanting mantras, and guided meditation have precisely this effect: telling yourself what you want so that you start believing it and it unconsciously guides your actions.

You can use this for your own journey by actively and consciously repeating these helpful beliefs. For a particularly crucial task or test of courage, you can also reformulate your belief and repeat it to yourself regularly and often.

Your aim is to weaken the beliefs that sabotage your courage as much as possible, preferably by eliminating them from your mind completely. This usually doesn't happen from one day to the next. Your brain has repeated this so often, this "neural highway" is perhaps six lanes wide, and without a speed limit you'll fall into the "it's not necessary/I can't do this/I'm not entitled to this/I've never been able to..." – trap. Identifying these beliefs is the beginning, and then you consciously replace them with the beliefs that strengthen your life-serving resolve.

Beliefs are not truths. They reduce the complexity of the world to a simple denominator for us and are "simplifiers" in our day-to-day decisions. Most of the time, there's nothing wrong with that. They are the result of social conventions ("trust is good, control is better"), educational experiences ("I'm too lazy/stupid/loud/shy/ambitious/egoistic/dreamy" – take your pick), or even an incisive experience (once bitten by a dog – every dog bites).

My client works at the second management level in a large corporation with a correspondingly high level of responsibility and there is a lot of competition among managers. One of her colleagues makes suggestions to their boss about wanting to take over my client's specialist areas, he discusses things intensively with the client's employees and spends a lot of time with them. My client perceives these actions as scheming, threatening, and deceitful. She has the feeling that he is alienating her team from her and inserting himself into her area of expertise. She feels helpless in this situation. When I ask her about her options, she comes up with a few, but for many of them she starts or ends with "I'm not allowed to do that." A wonderful belief: "I am not allowed to do that!" And this sentence pushes her into defenselessness. In the end, we found options that met her high ethical standards and enabled her to put a stop to her colleague's actions:

She spoke to her boss about her responsibilities, who then confirmed this in a team meeting with the rogue colleague present. She learned to speak to him about transgressions, to listen to his perspective and realized that he was so uncomfortable about her just bringing it up that he stopped his behavior. He must have thought he could simply take over her space without her noticing or defending herself. He was wrong.

Handling Mistakes Courageously

"I was once principal of the international school in Frankfurt. Of course, I also met children who went to a German school," the principal of our daughters' American school tells me.

> I often asked these children from the German school what they were particularly proud of and to show me. The children always showed me work in which they had no or almost no mistakes. The error-free dictation, the correctly calculated arithmetic problems. That's the German school system. When I ask the children at my school the same thing, they bring me a poem, or a picture, or a poster for a project they have worked on. That is our pedagogical system.

I have never forgotten this conversation, which took place in 2002. From my own time at school in Germany and on our return to Germany, I was able to retrace what she had said. Early in the German school system, we learn that it's best not to make mistakes. That we'll get an "A" in most subjects if we don't. And the more mistakes you make, the worse you are. This intolerance to mistakes makes sense for many tasks: where routines and standards have been developed and reliably and efficiently lead to the desired result. There are areas of life without fault tolerance: heart surgery, nuclear power plants, and flying airplanes. In many other areas of life, however, these standards and routines do not exist. Either they need to be developed, or they are not necessary at all, because the subject defies standards and routines. This is the case with all creative achievements – and in human interaction. Our fear of making mistakes can prevent us from discovering new things, experimenting, or even risking "getting emotionally involved."

For many times in life, there is no formula or dictionary with one correct answer – design, creativity, and trial and error are the order of the day.

The exacerbation of the fear of making mistakes is often called "perfectionism." People try not to make any mistakes to thus become unassailable. A futile endeavor. No one is "flawless" and can do everything outstandingly. Anyone who doesn't admit to their mistakes has inhuman expectations of themselves. Even if you can do something extraordinarily well, something can always go wrong. Whether it's an own goal in professional football, a stuttering newsreader, a stumbling Oscar winner: it's all part of life. The life-serving attitude toward this reality is a friendly acknowledgment of your own imperfections. Shake it off and carry on.

There are managers who spend a lot of energy searching for and correcting errors. They actively look for them, discuss them at length, and never seem to forget them. I say that fixing mistakes is leadership for beginners – more on this later in the book. These "Leadership beginners" have little ideas for the future, don't develop an overarching strategy, and see their added value in making sure their team doesn't make mistakes. What do you do when you come up against a boss who's like this? How can you muster courage? Of course, you can increase your level of "meticulousness" and accuracy, which will also make you more efficient. Remain calm when your boss points out a mistake, acknowledge, and correct it. And then talk about something more important as quickly as possible, e.g., how the project as a whole is progressing, how team members are developing, what your internal customers need from you, and how you have a great idea for exactly that. In this way, you can help both your boss and you to focus precious energy on more rewarding topics than looking for mistakes.

Acceptance, Forgiveness, and Self-Love

Acceptance: what has been, is done. You can no longer change it. But – you can decide what you make of it. "What if" – mind games leave you stuck in the past, let you wallow in mistakes, and tie up your energy instead of doing the next best thing.

"What am I going to do with it?" is much more life-serving than "How could this happen to me?" Accepting an unpleasant result or a difficult situation does not mean that you think it's good or resign yourself to it. However, you stop channeling energy into anger, disappointment, and frustration and put it into the "What now?" instead.

Forgiveness: Holding grudges requires holding on, spending energy on the past. We all get hurt and hurt other people. To varying degrees, by accident or on purpose, we hurt each other, and sometimes even ourselves. To forgive, you empathize with the other person's story and recognize your possible role in it. By forgiving, you leave behind the victim role and find agency how to handle the pain. Can you forgive everything? I can't. There are a few transgressions that still make my heart pound, awaken my flight or fight instinct, and I wish that the "perpetrators" would be punished somehow. Can I forgive a lot? Yes. I understood a lot of painful things, recognized my role in them, and also saw how the system in which we operated enabled hurtful behavior.

> To err is human, to forgive divine.
>
> Alexander Pope

To note: Forgiveness is a personal choice, not an obligation. Statements, such as "You have to forgive them," are brutal transgressions, often formulated by people who have not experienced the pain themselves and do not want to recognize the other's pain. Now, on to self-love: your capacity to be loving and appreciative of yourself. Missed opportunities, harsh criticism, or a failed project can invite you to condemn and belittle yourself and feel guilt or shame. If you recognize such a pattern for yourself – i.e., having a very punitive, negative, and even hurtful inner monologue whenever you make a "mistake" – then actively counter this with an attitude of acceptance, forgiveness, and appreciation. Turn the hurtful monologue into curiosity: What led to this missed opportunity? What do I want to change? What do I want to do in the future instead?

"What do I want to do in the future and who do I want to be?" and "What does the world need me for?" are questions in the chapter "Camp Future." They invite you to be self-loving: If I have landed on this earth as this being, in this body, at this time, that is a unique miracle I can celebrate every day and to which I want to give meaning. To this end, I recommend the precious book, The Choice by Dr. Edith Eger, in which the author, a Holocaust survivor, links her personal story of acceptance, forgiveness, and self-love with her work as a psychologist.

Your Courageous Mindset

You can develop a *courageous mindset* yourself. With your *courage bookkeeping*, you can visualize how much courage you already have and have had in your life. With *inner beliefs* that strengthen you in your abilities and your effectiveness, you give yourself courage. In your inner dialog, you give less and less airtime to beliefs that make you feel small and weak. When you start to see *mistakes as part of learning* and not as an indictment of your person, you have more energy for courageous decisions. A mindset of *acceptance, forgiveness, and self-love* releases energy mobilizing your power for future opportunities.

Chapter 6

Encouragement(s) for the Special Moments

There are those typical moments when fear arises, and you wish you had more tools available than the previously explored "hands on belly" exercise and stepping through the courage zone.

There are many effective ways to strengthen your courage: with the reflection method described in this chapter, you practice keeping the drama, the situation, your role, and the available opportunity apart and thus escape the paralyzing repetition of the head cinema faster.

From Drama to Opportunity

Do you have perpetual drama? Head cinema? Recounting the events? Thinking about how it happened? Discussing who or what is to blame? We humans love drama, and our brains are trained to engage in mental theater and rustling about. Save that it leads to so little. We stir and stir the familiar mush – and nothing ever really changes. The only change is the hardening of existing assessments and judgments. Courage doesn't need hardening, it wants a new beginning, a change, a departure. How do you get out of the drama, the ever-repeating stage play, and find ways to move forward, to change?

In a training course with Alan Seale, leadership expert, coach, and author, I learned a very helpful concept, which I use in many coaching and training sessions: the Four Levels of Engagement, coined as the D(i)SCO model (Seale, 2018). According to this model, every human interaction can be considered on four different levels: drama, situation, choice, and opportunity.

The first level: this is where drama reigns. We are at the level of appearances and ask the question of guilt and blame. With the answer the guilty are found, judgments are made, and the greatest courage needed here is the remorse of whoever is deemed "guilty." On the drama stage, our thoughts and conversations revolve around "he said, she said; I forgot; how could they, what an idiot" and so on. The energy goes into the question: "Who

DOI: 10.4324/9781003582724-7

or what is to blame for what happened?" As you can probably see for yourself, this mind movie can keep you quite busy and the result is usually pitifully small compared to the time and emotional effort involved. Nothing happens here except the assignment of guilt, having a bad conscience, and consolidating judgments.

The second level: we look at the circumstances and mechanisms that gave way to the drama. We may find new solutions, apply them, and – hopefully – avoid drama in the future. All solutions result from error prevention, not from future opportunities and requirements. You are already looking for more systematic explanations. "How could it come to this? And how do we get the situation under control?" The situation is analyzed, and you look at how the participants in this system can act in the future. But the system itself is not up for debate. This is somewhat more productive than the drama, but you are still in the situation and are not yet questioning your options for action. If you want to achieve more, you go to the next level.

The third level: you begin questioning your own role in what has happened and take courage to perhaps move differently in the future. You change your relationship to what has happened. By deciding to take on a different role in the future, you can ensure lasting change. Now ask yourself: "What, up until now, were my choices in this drama, this situation, and what role will I take on now instead, what is my intention moving forward?" Understanding your previous role can be very, very enlightening. Take, for example, a manager with a rather slothful team without much visible initiative. What image of leadership, what attitudes and behaviors does the manager show, and would the employees perhaps be more active if they changed something? Give more freedom, praise more, trust more? Actively invite for differing point of views? Things get really exciting when you enter the fourth level of observation.

The fourth level: I call it the oxygen tent, where you get a lot of air to breathe again. You leave guilt, the accusations, the retelling, and the eternal pattern of action and reaction behind. You look to the future. What happened, happened. What matters more is what comes next! With an active search for opportunities, the drama loses its power, and the underlying forces become accessible and usable. Whether you find yourself in a Solo Drama and understand the forces at work or you're in a casted play with others, in a difficult situation, everyone communicates about the opportunities: suddenly, you are guided by images of the future instead of searching for guilt and avoiding mistakes. Your conversations have more energy, you find better solutions, and courage has a chance. That's when the manager mentioned above might notice how much the team members need encouragement, training, or clearer roles in order to work more actively and creatively.

You may feel your perspective shift as you read this, and you may notice a physical change from tension to breathing more easily again as you trace your way through the different levels. "What opportunity does this offer us?" is a bold question. The answers may lead you out of your comfort zone, invite new solutions and ideas, and demand creativity. If you want to bring more opportunity focus in your life, you can use the questions in the box "Opportunity Discovery" as a tool.

Opportunity Discovery

Take the first drama of the day and immediately jump to the third stage with the question:

- What is my relationship to what is going on?
- What roles exist and which one do I choose?

That's where the first surprises may come.

- How many roles do you see?
- And what happens when you claim a new one?
- Is that possible? How does your environment react?

You can go on:

- What opportunities arise from the drama?
- Can you figure this out on your own or do you explore with another person?
- What do you do next?

You can start an expedition like this every day. Look back at the end of the week:

- What have you learned?
- What took a lot of courage?
- What was easy?
- Will you continue next week?

The Magic of "No"

Yes, there are many opportunities to mobilize courage so we may shape our lives according to our will. Sometimes we need courage to distance ourselves from the wishes and demands of others. How do you balance your needs and those of others? When are you being selfish and when are the demands of others driving you up the wall? The dilemma: the better you become, the more will be asked of you. As long as you continue to deliver, more demands will come, since it works – for the others. But what of you? What falls by the wayside? Restful sleep, time with friends, an enjoyable walk? Or do you not even get to realize the projects important to you, as you are too busy helping others realize theirs? If you make them yours – that's fine. But if you progressively give up your dreams, what you want to achieve, how you want to live – then maybe it's time to learn the magical powers of the word "no."

Your "no's" to external demands create your very own profile. Without saying "no," you simply become the result of the impact of external forces on you. Your "no's" are an expression of your priorities, strengths, and concerns. They create your profile. "Yeses" are overtime, exhaustion, and frustration. "Yeses" fulfill the wishes of others.

A manifesto for saying "no":

- Many a "no" is necessary to say a big "yes"
- I like to fulfill wishes – including mine
- "No" is one of my options
- "No" does not take away goodwill, acceptance, or love
- I register emotional harassment in response to my "no" and it does not guide my further actions
- A "no" avoids the frustration of not experiencing gratitude and reciprocity
- I can take my time to answer

Sometimes your "yes" comes from an unspoken expectation of reciprocity, of gratitude. If you don't sense gratitude from your counterpart, you may build up resentment. Do they know about your expectations? And are they really willing to fulfill them? There, as an example, is an editor-in-chief, who relies on one editor in particular as a permanent rescue center. Whatever is left unfinished or unpleasant to deal with goes to this editor. They work late into the night and do the "homework" their boss gave them over the weekend. They never contradict them and fulfill all their wishes because there's a promise: "As soon as the opportunity arises, I'll promote you." Then the boss leaves for another station. The successor doesn't know about the promise, isn't interested in it, and does not promote the editor. The editor is left with disappointment, frustration, and anger and feels like a victim. Stories like these occur countless times and in all kinds of constellations, for sure you have observed them yourself – or had a part in them? Connecting with what you need, and what boundaries you want to set can change the constellation in your favor.

The more frequently you accept the demands of others, your "yeses" for your own needs weaken. Your goals become eroded by the wishes and dictates of others. If you keep saying "yes," it can lead you to systematic overload. If you are looking for acknowledgment and belonging by saying "yes," stop for a moment: is it really true that you'll only receive acceptance, affirmation, and appreciation if you never tell the people around you "no"? If it were, doesn't that reveal more about those people than you? That's one big question. The other is: If you accept, affirm, and appreciate yourself – does a "no" fall easier from your lips?

How do you say "no"? Learn to negotiate. First, listen to what is expected of you. Ask questions, understand the request, and have the other confirm that they feel understood. Only then do you compare their demand with your existing plans, commitments, and deadlines. The negotiation starts: on timing, on scope, on who is doing what, and perhaps on a reward. I suggest never let go of a "no" as an option, it gives you space for finding the best path for all involved. Look at the manifesto for saying "no," it wants to empower you.

Ways to say "no":

- "No" or "No, thank you"
- "That doesn't suit me at the moment, please try again some other time"
- "How nice of you to ask me, unfortunately, I can't do it right now"
- "I can't do what you're asking in full at this point in time. Is it enough for you if I do... until...?"
- "I understand that you want... from me

I don't want to do that, and I won't."

In some situations, you will be more verbose and diplomatic. Just stay honest.

Your "no" is not a "no" to the person making the request, but a "yes" to the business strategy or to the promises you have already made. And a "yes" may also reflect a promise to yourself, to do what is important to you.

Ah – and here comes the fear: they think you're lazy, they don't think you're committed enough – you want to do everything expected of you, etc. Fine. Then do overtime, do things you think are wrong and get increasingly angry while you're doing them. Anxiety and fear are rather wretched mentors.

Your Body Can Help You

I was about to welcome "my" conference. More than 100 colleagues and employees from all over the world were sitting in the auditorium, awaiting an inspiring, energetic, and substantial presentation from me, the global director. And me? I was completely exhausted, drained, and frustrated. For weeks I had been contemplating whether I would really go on stage or throw in the towel last minute. My narcissistic bosses, intrigues between department heads, a constant, unproductive back-and-forth on big projects – this is how I had been experiencing my work environment lately and it had cost me (almost) all my strength to get to this point. And yet, I went on stage with the intention of giving my colleagues energy, direction, and confidence. Afterward, people came up to me and congratulated me on the best performance they had ever seen from me in this company. What had happened? On the eve of the conference, I had thorough conversations with my colleagues who had traveled there. They told me about their successes, the great collaboration with my team, and their faith in our new strategy. On the morning of my appearance, I decided to put the performance of my management team, the work of my people, and my role in the company first. I wanted to take responsibility for the results and to not let my team down. I found my courage and wanted to go through with my "performance." And then I allowed my body to help me. Backstage, I was jumping around and swinging my arms. On stage, I stood with my shoulders back, straightened spine, smiling, and standing steady on both feet, with my hands loosely clasped together. I deliberately spoke in a low voice, a tick slower than I usually like – and my body said: "All right, we're doing it." And that was it. If you need courage, your body can help you.

What does your body do when you act courageously? How does your voice sound, how is your body tension, how do you use the space? Where do your eyes look? Observe, and let your body be courageous. Stand up when you make a difficult phone call, speak in a deeper and slower voice, and stand firmly. When your body behaves confidently, the neurons in your head calm down too!

When a situation "tips over" – you notice feeling anxious, a tinge of panic – your body can help. If your brain goes into panic mode, avoid trying to be particularly clever or witty. Your brain is busy being afraid and has no extra brain capacity for analysis, diplomacy, or the next presentation slide. Instead, concentrate on your breathing and exhale longer than you inhale to calm your heart. Do this a couple of times. Concentrate on everything happening around you. Notice sounds, things, smells, etc. If possible, place a hand on your heart (once again) and gently tap the center of your chest. Give your anxious brain fresh, real sensory impressions. Just breathe and give your amygdala time to calm down. Try to smile, which signals to your body that everything is okay. You can also have a drink or stand up and walk a few steps until the physical anxiety subsides.

You can also "prepare your body for courage" before particularly important and unsettling situations: for at least 2 minutes and wherever you are unobserved, adopt a posture that feels strong and courageous. Concentrate on your courage, your will, and your prospects. Maintain your position and thoughts for two minutes. Then, you go into a difficult situation. You will appear and potentially become more powerful, more determined, and confident.

Visualizing "After Courage"

"STOP!" our riding instructor, Lisa, called out. When our horses stood still, she continued: "Next, I will call you up one by one and the first movement of each horse will be a canter jump." We all laughed out loud. We were all experienced riders, but getting a horse from a standing start into a canter jump – none of us had ever tried that before and it sounded like a massive challenge. Cathrin gave us some help:

> Each of you can do it. The horses can do it too. You must want to do it and communicate that to your horse. To do this, you need to be totally focused and anticipate the canter jump in your mind. Imagine how you shift your weight, how you give the horse canter aids and then imagine this jump. Then it will work.

When it was my turn, I followed Lisa's instructions, and it turned out she was right. It worked. It was both a triumphant and perplexing feeling that I can still recall today. Since then, I have used this technique of inner visualization for countless situations that are arduous for me. By playing through the situation internally, I become more confident, I am more aware of what I have to do – and my inclination to act courageously grows.

How do you do that? Take some time, find a calm moment, and create as vivid a mental picture as possible of what you will achieve if you act with courage. Use all your senses: Can you feel happiness in your stomach? What posture are you taking? Who else is there? What are they doing?

What are you saying? How wide is your smile? Or are you laughing with joy? The more intense and "sensory-rich" your imagination is, the more "hooks" you create for your brain to memorize this goal. It's best if you create a symbol, perhaps with a certain word, gesture, or melody, which you can call up again to mobilize your courage.

The Right Timing

Big annual planning meeting at Procter & Gamble. Our managing director – I'll call him Jonathan* – towers over the meeting, around 25 people in the room, team by team presenting their marketing plans and budget requirements. The atmosphere is tense, Jonathan wants to see small budgets with big impact (no surprise here). He repeatedly demands changes to the plans. Courageous colleagues object, there is a brief exchange of blows, each time Jonathan "wins." The CEO is a very clever and thoughtful person who can be persuaded by good arguments. But not and never in front of a large audience. He wants to display his unchallenged authority and comprehensive expertise. This is not a good time for courage. At the next one-on-one meeting, I present my arguments, we discuss various budget scenarios, and I leave with a serious and well-thought-out plan. For my goal – to have enough budget and people for my tasks – I didn't need to win in front of a large audience. I just needed the go-ahead from my boss, and I had looked for and found the right situation.

If you want something that requires your courage, how can you choose a situation that makes it as easy as possible?

After falling ill with COVID, my coachee Paul* returns to work. In the first team meeting he attends, his boss reprimands him for not attending meetings during his illness. A little bit later, he requests holiday leave, and she demands that he take his laptop with him and be constantly available. To Paul, this behavior is really crossing boundaries, and his relationship with his boss, whom he otherwise appreciates, suffers. He wants to redraw his boundaries and in our coaching session, we think about how he can go about it. He decides to discuss his desire for respect after his recovery and for an undisturbed vacation in a video conference (she is in New York; he is in London). He'll make an appointment with her – so he won't have to wait for a chance meeting to clarify his needs. Others describe her as "terrifying," and Paul finds a way to manage her energy: since she tends to get very loud, even shouting, and this quickly throws him off balance, he decides to turn the volume down low in the video chat. In addition, he will make her picture on the screen very small.

What I find so important about this example – Paul didn't react in the same moment the boundaries were crossed. We've all been there, haven't we? We would all like to have quick wits or the diplomatic skills to turn a situation in our favor immediately. But it doesn't always work, you may be too flustered, thrown off balance, and you stay silent. That's not a bad thing. You move ahead by asking for a meeting, you bring up the topic and talk about how to work together better.

Ouch, That Hurts! or Does It?

Courage is "seeing danger and proceeding anyway," and sometimes it goes wrong. In my personal "courage accounting," I have discovered that the negative consequences that I have experienced when I failed despite my courage have to do with my innermost needs: those for human connection, for creative power, and for lasting contribution. And all these failed efforts hurt badly and at some point, became part of my life narrative – as a great realization, as acceptance, as self-understanding. During the only sacking of my life, the restructuring director told me, among other things: "You have very high standards for your work, and I don't think we need them here." Hmmm. A dismissal is humiliating, frightening, and unsettling. And to this day I wish it hadn't happened because I'd rather leave myself than be let go. Ouch. That hurts.

Or does it? Despite all the pain of departing, a shattered team, and destroyed work – my insights into corporate life and career injunctions, about good and not-so-good bosses, about enmities and friendships are first-hand and true. I was able to understand how I act under massive pressure (nervous, true to my values, constantly in danger of hurting my own interests) and what hurts me (loss of relationships, destruction of my work, and lack of recognition). I have observed how people in complex organizations act under massive pressure (self-protecting, fearful, some paralyzed, and others very agile and skillful). Now, I know these dynamics, can work with them, and make these insights benefit my clients. Of course, it happens to me that I relive these difficult hours, days, and weeks, and feel miserable and fallible again: failed courage leads us into dark moments. Stepping out of these loops is what's important since I can no longer change what has happened – the experience is now part of my life, and I'll use it for my future life. That's what courage is worth.

Moments of Courage

With the *DSCO method*, you can put a stop to the mind games, the constant loops, and find your commitment for courage: instead of reviewing what has happened ("drama"), you look at the circumstances ("situation"), then decide what role ("choice") you want to play in the event and focus on the future possibilities ("opportunity") that arise. In this way, you mobilize energy for the future instead of crying over spilt milk.

Sometimes you need courage to do your own thing and not fulfill the wishes and demands of others. There are many moments when *saying "no" is courageous*, right, and important.

Mobilize your body so that it shows you and others courageous actions with its positive tension and posture. Another tool in such moments is *visualization*: your thoughts create an inner film of the results of your courage: this image of success literally propels you over the difficult hurdles, and releases the energy it takes to be courageous.

Courage also needs the *right timing*. Perhaps you need a little preparation for the critical conversation, or you suspect that your boss will listen to you more openly at lunch than in a team meeting, or vice versa. Give your courage a chance by timing it right.

Reference

Seale, A. (2018). *Transformational presence: The tools, skills and frameworks*. Center for Transformational Presence.

Chapter 7

Your Courage and Others

We humans are social beings. Many of our fears are related to our connection to others, how you are perceived and how people behave toward you. Let's talk about how courage can play out in our social life.

Respect from the Harvard Professor

Completely stunned and shocked I realized I had lost again. In our management training at Vassar College, we were playing a negotiation game. It was a standard game from game theory. In the game, everyone in the group announces how they are betting in each round. Then everyone bets face down. After everyone has bet, the bets are revealed. If everyone sticks to the agreement, everyone gets points. If only one person sticks to the agreement, that person loses massively and everyone else gains a few points. The instruction was: win for your team. Now I thought I knew the game. I had played it years earlier in another company. Back then, it had gone like this: for the first two rounds, nobody stuck to the agreement, and everyone lost. Then the most analytically gifted and socially courageous explained what we were doing was nonsense. If everyone sticked to the agreement, everyone would win, and the total payout would be greater.

From this moment onward, everyone kept to their agreement. It made sense for everyone, both financially and culturally. But in this training, I was in a different organization. Seemingly, the people were not as analytical, and the culture was different, too. Despite being shown a video by the CEO on trust-based negotiation before the game, most of my teammates broke their promise every round. Except me. Because I expected them to realize that this was mathematical nonsense. But due to my excitement, frustration, and insecurity, I wasn't able to explain and communicate this properly, so I ended up with an epochal "bad" score – visible to everyone on the score sheet hanging on the wall (my heart still beats faster today when thinking about it). There were quite a few people who looked at me with pity and probably thought I was a complete idiot when it came to negotiations. But then something

DOI: 10.4324/9781003582724-8

happened: the Harvard professor who led the game, and wrote a standard work on negotiation, congratulated me on my behavior, and said that he had never seen something like it before. Afterward, a few people came up to me and thanked me for doing what they didn't have the courage to do themselves. What had happened? Had I really been courageous? First, I thought, it's just a silly game, it's about a few points on a wall, I don't need to lie to my colleagues' faces for that. Second, I considered my values and felt like I had to choose between "honesty," "team spirit" and "success." Again, I chose honesty, with the aim to be trustworthy. If I had known beforehand how exhausting it would be, I would have likely made a different choice and eased through this game unnoticed and blissfully ignorant of what I should do. Something else happened, too: after a certain point in the game, I was no longer brave but simply helpless and frustrated. Every one of my explanations of the game bounced off my peers, I became more and more nervous, headless to the point I couldn't even do the math anymore. That's what it's like when the amygdala takes over the brain and only cares about bare survival. That's when the center for computing disconnects. And from then onward, I no longer realized that I was losing, but instead believed rather diffusedly that it would still "go well." In the end, I felt stupid and naive. So, the score of the game was a disaster for me, but for some people, I was the "match winner" in terms of ethical behavior. What is this anecdote about? Not everything that looks like courage to others is courageous for the person doing it. However, it can still be good.

"Just Shut Up for Once!"

Caroline* is constantly annoyed by a colleague and wants to learn how to deal with this in a coaching session. This colleague really annoys her. She describes his behavior in meetings with clients at their large law firm:

> He talks way too much, repeats himself, even interrupts me or repeats exactly what I've already said and acts as if he's the first to ever say it. It makes a really bad impression, and I think he wants to prove to everyone around that he's better than me.

I invite Caroline to tell me what she would like to say to him. Here we go:

> We have to make a good impression in front of our customers. We want to appear mature, intelligent, and well prepared. You babble for the sake of babbling. And then you repeat yourself and what I already said. It comes across as agitated and immature. You need to be concise, to the point. Besides, it's clear, I'm taking the lead. And then you just shut up for once.

This might be abbreviated, but it's the essence of Caroline's irritations, judgments, and attacks.

We switch roles. She takes the role of her colleague and listens to the same words from my mouth. At first, she seems satisfied: "That's exactly how it is." Then she turns thoughtful. How will her colleague feel, what will he do? We talk about the effect of judgments, and how they put distance between us instead of finding common ground. And how important it is to be clear about your own needs when you have intensely negative feelings as she does toward her colleague.

Suddenly she says:

> Now I know how I'll do it. I'll say: I want to get better at my work. Can you please help me? I want to practice being very approachable in conversations with customers, getting straight to the point and getting by without repeating myself. It would also be good if you didn't interrupt me, would that be okay with you? Could you help me and give me some feedback after the meeting as to whether I succeeded?

Caroline's energy has completely shifted. Positive, open, and curious about how the other person will react. At the beginning, she wanted to "just get rid of everything" upsetting her. Understandable after all that pent-up anger, though it just doesn't bring that much change. Now she has a clear intention, is in touch with her need to learn, and can go into the conversation very openly.

Things often take so much courage because we simply approach controversies in the wrong way. We go into confrontation with accusations, judgments, and demands that we may have already played out in our heads for hours, days, or weeks. We immerse ourselves in drama, in judgment, hurt, disappointment, anger, and rage. All parties to the conflict feel attacked, perhaps threatened – the battle begins and is perhaps ended with a compromise or a victory. And what remains is a strained, negative relationship. In such a dispute, "courage" consists of asserting oneself, positioning one's own judgment as "true" and very often weakening the other party. This aggressiveness feels courageous to some – because aggressive behavior is not in the comfort zone. However, aggression in and of itself is not necessarily part of the growth zone and can be very destructive for us and others.

Progressive Communication

With Caroline, we practiced out "progressive communication," which is taught in many team-coaching sessions, in political conflicts and schools. Marshall Rosenberg developed the concept (he called it "non-violent communication") in the 1980s and I use it a lot to improve rigid and negative relationships. This approach can bring relationships into the growth zone. Even if the bad relationship doesn't feel like a "comfort zone," it does take courage to step out of the mechanisms of said relationship.

Using the approach developed by Rosenberg, you seek to talk to the other person to first establish a mutual understanding. Only when this has been achieved can solutions be found. With progressive communication, you first gain clarity about yourself: What need of yours is being violated by the situation/behavior of others? How does this affect you? What would you like to experience in the future? The last answer shapes your request to the other person. What may feel formulaic and artificial at first can be a real game changer in your relationships if you communicate without judgment and don't blame the other person for your feelings.

In progressive communication, you describe the situation that triggered the conflict with the other person as objectively as possible, as if a video camera was recording everything you say. You then explain what effect it had on you and what need of yours was violated. Before you can do this, you ought to clarify for yourself which need has been damaged. This inner recognition alone will do you good. And then say what you would like and ask the other person whether they would fulfill this request. Whether they do, and to what extent, is up to them; you can't give orders.

In our coaching session, Caroline focused on formulating the third and fourth steps, and that can sometimes be enough. In principle, this approach can completely change a conflict. The prerequisite is you consciously shift toward a cooperative and respectful attitude. In this approach, you take responsibility for your needs, your feelings, and your reactions to the behavior of others. And you are empathetic to the needs and feelings of the other person. You do not judge or condemn the other person's actions but clearly articulate how these actions infringed on your needs. The genius of this method: you agree on respective needs and discuss future actions that fulfill them as far as possible. The premise of the conversation is that all needs are legitimate and non-negotiable. Collisions with others can only occur when it comes to strategies for fulfillment, and these can be negotiated.

What does progressive communication have to do with courage?

We often confuse "attacking" with "being brave" – when we finally let someone have it all: our judgments, frustrations, and negative feelings flung at their face. When we go on the attack, we "dare to do something." We long to overcome this bad situation our relationship is in and then we just let it rip. Progressive communication does not seek escalation for your courage, but real understanding of and with other people. For many people, becoming aware of their own needs and revealing them to the other person is a step out of their comfort zone. At the same time, this step can also enable their inner honesty, giving them the strength to look for a good solution.

Plotting, Scheming, Toxicity

Unfortunately, you are not alone if you suffer from and in your work environment. Second: make something of it. I am firmly convinced that if all employees suffering from mean-spirited colleagues and incompetent bosses were to address this behavior consciously and purposefully, we would all benefit from it. Yes, I know that there is a power imbalance between you and your boss. And how helpless you can feel when someone seems to be out to get you. Toxic people look for faults and culprits, make and spread judgments, and like to expose others with their "weaknesses."

I also know that I can feed the beast of fear, disparagement, and disrespect. Or, instead, mobilize a different energy of kindness, objectivity, and trust. It works. Really. Not always but quite often.

Who finds whom difficult and what makes us suffer varies from person to person. Sometimes the chemistry doesn't seem to be there, sometimes more, sometimes not at all. Whether we trigger feelings of irritation or even threat in others can be independent of our good intentions. An unreturned phone call goes unnoticed by one co-worker, and the other feels unseen and deeply disrespected. While the action is the same, its impact on two people can be fundamentally different.

What is courageous in your dealings with others, how do you find the way to positive energy when you find yourself or your team being the target of attacks? Here are some tips:

- Find opportunity in what is happening. What can you learn, how can you use the situation to your advantage? As difficult as it may feel at first – look for a gift in difficult circumstances
- "Who do I want to be, how do I want to come across?" Your answers to these questions offer you a new attitude and options for action
- Ask what's going on. Whether you did something that irritated or upset the other person. Listen to them, ask questions to understand the hurt. Maybe you want to explain yourself, or express your regret, or just leave it at that. Just asking can put an end to your inner mental gymnastics because you now know what is going on
- Find common interests. What does the other person want to achieve that is also important to you? Can you join forces?
- Reduce the time you spend together. If nothing helps and there is no rapprochement or understanding, limit the exchanges to the bare minimum, don't expect more than there is, and avoid giving the other person more energy than necessary

- Don't try to change the other person. You can only control your reaction to the other person, not their impulses
- Instead of getting upset, practice staying calm. Count to 10, 100, 500, or a million. The person will not change. You can only change how you experience them. Who knows what that's good for
- Be prepared in case of repeated targeted attacks, humiliations, and judgments. Analyze the attack, its energy, its intention, and its effect on you and others. Be careful not to bottle it all up. Have a confidant, perhaps a professional coach, with whom you can talk through what has happened, again limit the time you spend on this – the mind games tie up your energy, keep you in conflict, and are not beneficial to your life. Focus on things that you like and that are good for you

> Another important tip: contemplate and identify your own feelings but don't give in to them:
>
> "Oh, there is fear" not "I am fearful." "Oh, there is anger," not "I am angry." This helps you to take more conscious action.

If your whole team is affected by this dynamic, turn toward your purpose, image of success, strategy, and the tasks you can accomplish together. Focusing on concrete results will allow you to develop professional pride as a team and individually, even in a difficult environment.

Sometimes, all your resolve for great work and trustful leadership is not enough. The interests and decisions of those with more power than you lead somewhere else than you would like. How can you deal with that if you find yourself in such a situation?

Find out whether you think this is an isolated, short-term problem. How long can you cope and what protection can you build up for yourself? Can you create space to act fearlessly, respectfully, and sustainably? Then do so and see how your example and your results have a positive effect.

Are all the signals flashing red? Has this been company culture for a long time, is this how the powerful players behave, protecting each other and punishing anyone who seems to resist? Then protect yourself, mobilize confidants and allies to give you support in difficult situations, and check whether you can and want to go somewhere else.

What is courageous here? I don't have a general answer. Looking back at my own key moments, I think:

Sometimes it's okay to keep quiet. The waves are too high, the current is too strong, emotions are far too heated to express any dissent. I would trigger a short circuit that, in the end, would serve no-one or rather blow up in at least one person's face. Even if I could make a fiery speech, have a heroine moment – I don't do it. I tolerate some things that I would do differently, leave my mark where I can, and make sure that my decisions allow me to keep looking the person in the mirror in the eyes. My moment will come, sooner or later.

"Or later" is okay – as long as "later" doesn't become "never"! Sometimes it took me much longer than I wanted before I made the switch. But luckily, I think I ultimately made the leap every time. I don't think staying, even though you're constantly twisting yourself to others' wishes, is beneficial to your life.

In cases of acute abuse of power or overstepping boundaries, you should seek a direct conversation, speak to the next higher level, or call the complaints hotline. In some cases, I'd also advise you to consult with a lawyer because the toxic behavior is relevant under employment law. And sometimes you reach the point where you put all your energy into your job search. Sleepless nights, anxiety, and depression are not conducive to life, and if they continue, they'll take their toll on your mental and physical health. Only once did I have to make an official complaint in my professional life. In a conversation with a higher-ranking person, I was threatened, humiliated, and insulted. The person carried out their attacks in such a targeted, cool, and considered manner that I was convinced it wasn't the first time and apparently, he had gotten away with it so far (which the HR manager later confirmed to me). At first, I was just shocked by all that was said and the intent behind the attack – to silence and isolate me from my boss and close colleagues by telling on them. Then I looked at my options, spoke to my boss, and decided to bring an official complaint. I wanted to see a manager like that sanctioned and I could only achieve that if I spoke up. I knew that there would probably be no sanctioning and my position in the company would be weakened. Because I was so unclouded about my needs – to be a credible, respected voice in the company and to work loyally with my boss and colleagues - I was able to take this step.

And who of us stayed in their place? The bully. I was new, without an internal network and my courage was greater than the principles of the organization. But still, it was me, who moved on to bigger and better things!

In 2021, credible accusations were published about the management behavior of the editor-in-chief of the largest tabloid in Germany. There were allegations of abuse of power, sexual relations, despite the power imbalance, and drug use in the workplace. One article reported that those affected had indeed turned to the next level up, but that there had been no consequences to date. That is appalling. I imagine how much courage it must have taken for those women to approach the higher-ups, and then nothing happens. Ultimately, the editor-in-chief was dismissed, not because of the above accusations, but because he did not provide his employer with truthful information.

Of the Loneliness of the Brave

Everyone but me gets up hastily, everyone wants to get out the door as quickly as possible. We are an international leadership team and have just been told by the second-in-command that our boss is leaving the company (effective immediately), who their successor will be, that there will be a major reorganization, and that we should make ourselves available for one-on-one meetings. In non-corporate speech, the announcement of a bloodbath. But I don't want to get up or leave, yet. I still have a lot of questions. Above all, when and how our teams will be informed and what the next steps will be? I ask my colleagues to stop leaving and I pose my questions to the second-in-command. He is obviously irritated by my intervention. Yet, I get my questions answered, and we somewhat agree on how to proceed.

The next day, my colleague tells me: "Yesterday you were the only one with balls, and Antonio thinks the same." To this day, I still don't understand what she and Antonio found particularly brave. But I understood that others also found my behavior courageous, which may have further confirmed my dismissal in my one-on-one meeting. If someone says to you: "You're so brave" or "I would never dare to do that!" and you don't see it that way, you can ascertain three things: (1) What that person is afraid of. (2) You didn't see the risk and may have a blind spot and (3) You might be alone when things get uncomfortable, because the risk may be greater than you anticipated.

I would like to emphasize the latter. We often hear "You're brave" as an admiring compliment, sense allies or expect followers. This is a hasty reaction and the wrong conclusion. If someone says that to you, ask! What do you think is brave? How do you assess the situation? What risks do you see that I am not aware of? If I am so brave and it goes wrong, what will your role be, will you help me? The answers may offer you perspectives and insights you were missing before.

Find and Activate Allies

In this book, I would like to show you ways to find your own personal courage. But what role do other people play in this? In my experience, they play a huge role. Whether in your family, among friends, or in professional contexts – are you being encouraged there or do you wallow in your zone of comfort? Do you have friends who are happy about your courageous actions or show resentment and jealousy when you grow? Even though we can't freely choose every social interaction and some people in our lives are inescapable, you can influence the effect important people have on your courage.

My closest ally is Oliver, my husband. In over 40 years of life together, we started a family and lived in different countries and constellations (including me commuting between Paris and Minden and Amsterdam and Minden). Whether as students, career starters, up-and-comers, managers, or self-employed, we have always found a path we could walk together, and I have always been able to rely on his encouragement and support.

Nurture and care for the people who "believe in you," who encourage you again and again in important situations, who tend to your wounds "afterward" and stand by you no matter how much you might fail. Pay attention to who keeps discouraging you with sentences like "I would never dare to do that!", "Are you sure?", "You'll never manage that!", "I don't know if you can do that!".

Listen carefully to how these people react to your bold plans and intentions. Who wants to slow you down and what is their intention? Talk to the "brakemen" about your goals, why they are important to you and why you need encouragement. Ask for support and be specific about what that entails. You may tell them what slows you down and frustrates you and ask for their perspective. Have they understood you and do they want to support you in your choices?

If this person is important in your life and their attitude is decisive for your future courage, the conversation should continue. Understand the reasons. Does your courage perhaps trigger fear ("If you accept this great job, you'll have less time for the family, and everything will be up to me.")? Put plans together and make clear agreements. If a slowpoke wants to keep hitting the brakes – so be it. Decide what is important to you. Avoid judging others for their attitude. Concentrate on your goals and your scope for action.

I am happy and grateful to have people around me who, when in doubt, trust me more than I do and who give me courage when I have lost it. Yes, of course, I have met people who belittled me, criticized me nastily, and denied me my dreams. I don't want to take them with me on my life's journey. If I can, I simply break off contact (I can leave behind the condescending personnel consultant or the jovial fellow student or strike them from my address book). And if that doesn't work ("Wow, my boss doesn't trust me to do this!")? I prove what I can do and if possible change my environment and find a place to grow. All in all, it tended to work.

So much for your individual courage. With the reflections and exercises in the last chapters, you have expanded your scope of action, found new mindsets, and tried working with some helpful tools. In the next part of the book, I will focus on "courageous leadership" – how you can create an environment in which others can and want to act courageously.

Your Courage and Others

With *progressive communication*, you need (almost) no courage to deal with tensions and conflicts. Without assigning blame or making judgments, you can achieve better understanding and find new solutions with others. This is possible because you respect your and other's needs. This *respect reduces tension and aggression* and helps you to solve problems.

Courage can wither in a scheming, negative, aggressive environment. Use the D(i)SCO (Drama - Situation - Choice - Opportunity) model to stay out of drama. Focus on what you want and how you want to be. Stay true to yourself and don't let yourself burn out. If possible, find allies or a coach you can talk to so that you don't feel lonely.

In the second part of the book, we discuss how you can affect a social system so that the people operating in that system learn to behave more positively, openly, and collegially. Not everyone who admires your courage will be your ally. *Don't confuse admiration with alliance.*

Part 2

Courage in Organizations

Chapter 8

Leading for Courage

In the next few chapters, I will talk about how we can take responsibility for more courage in teams, organizations, and companies. How we can enable as many people as possible in our organization to act courageously and step out of their comfort zones for a common cause? I will be talking a lot about "leadership," by which I mean the capacity to move people. No more, no less. This can be a formal role with decision-making rights and accountability in a company. But it can also simply be your influence without formal "power," without titles, budgets, and other resources. The good thing is that if you can move people through formal or informal influence, you can advocate for more courage. This enables growth, change, and impact.

There are conditions that make it easier for people to be individually courageous. I talk about these in the following chapters and invite you to create and promote them in your environment. These are conditions, but no guarantees for more courage. Whether courage happens is decided in small moments, too. For example, when a person expresses their opinion, a colleague nods in agreement, a manager leans forward and seeks eye contact to offer support. Such small gestures can instill confidence, which strengthens courage.

The greater your influence – through your position or your personality – the more you can help people overcome their fear and act courageously. Courage is the capacity to overcome fear, even if the consequences are unpleasant, painful, or difficult to calculate. We need a lot of courage – in companies, organizations, and politics. We won't be able to overcome the monumental challenges that humanity has conjured up for itself by simply "carrying on."

In the first part, I discuss fundamental questions about courage in organizations – what is particularly difficult and especially necessary in today's world, what role leadership plays, and what the situation is regarding morality and responsibility. In an intermediate step, I describe the "fears in organizations" that I have encountered in my career in corporations, in

DOI: 10.4324/9781003582724-10

coaching executives, in business and politics in recent years. The third part is much more practical – I offer you systemic questions and tools for the courageous "constitution" of organizations with a "Compass for the Courageous Organization." In the fourth part, there are – analogous to the personal courage makers – organizational courage makers. Which collective mindset encourages, how you can lead courageously, what additional systemic levers there are, and how you can mobilize and control the courage to change.

Courage in a VUCA World

> I must choose between despair and energy? I choose the latter.
>
> John Keats

The world seems to be spinning faster and faster. Crises overlap and reinforce each other, dramatic events thwart bright plans – welcome to the "VUCA world," a world full of volatile, uncertain, complex, and ambiguous developments and events. The term was introduced in the US military at the beginning of the 1990s to describe the major global political, economic, and technological changes following the collapse of the Eastern Bloc and is currently used in many leadership training courses and management guides (USAHEC, 2022).

For organizations, the VUCA world means that the demands on leadership have changed massively, and we constantly must leave behind what we have learned and tried and tested in order to meet the challenges. But we don't know how to do this. It's difficult, it's scary. Courage is required because the consequences of our actions are difficult to predict, and fissures are constantly throwing wrenches into our works. Courage is also required because we need to say goodbye to old ideas of leadership. An image in which a manager has all the answers and can always say "which way is up" and has sufficient and correct knowledge along with all the necessary skills. That is no longer possible in the VUCA world. The pace is too fast, the range of issues is too broad, and more people are necessary to contribute to a solution. This is why I think it is so important to agree on a strong, binding compass within the organization, which can be used to continuously assess results, events, disruptions, and crises and agree on the next steps.

I would like to dig deeper into one aspect that I consider particularly important for the topic of "courage": complexity. In our everyday language, we often use the words "complex" and "complicated" interchangeably. In the term "VUCA," the "C" stands for "complex," not for "complicated," and you should know the difference and use it for your courageous actions.

Something is complicated, if it consists of multiple parts that are interrelated and calculable in those interrelations, though it may be difficult.

Even for a complicated problem, cause and effect can be clearly determined, though it can take a long time to find the correct formula and map the processes. Once the interrelationships have been defined, the actions can be agreed on and carried out, which then leads to the desired effect. Analyses, models, expert interviews, process definitions, Key Performance Indicators (KPIs) and Objectives and Key Results (OKRs) can all help to understand and control complicated phenomena. In essence, there is "one button to push" for all complicated phenomena, and most people find that wonderful.

Something is complex, if it is made up of two or more parts that are hard or impossible to unravel, study, or even solve. There are many interrelationships in complex situations. These are not or only partially calculable, and therefore, the results of actions are also difficult to predict. The various elements are often not "things," but human actors, individually or in organizations. In addition, there are environmental phenomena, such as climate catastrophe, the consequences of which scientists can calculate to some extent but will still repeatedly cause surprise disasters. The methods that work well for complicated problems are not sufficient for complex phenomena. The search for the "one button" is futile and, thus, frustrating. It often leads to tension, conflict, and despair among those affected.

It is courageous to recognize that you have left complicatedness and landed on a complexity. It is courageous to admit that many good methods will not suffice in a complex situation. It is courageous to agree on new ways to involve more people in consideration and action. It is courageous to point out the limitations of "believing in buttons" to all those who think they should "just make suggestions." It is courageous to muster the patience, diligence, and strength to address the entire phenomenon in such a way that truly sustainable strategies are found. This applies to climate catastrophe, armed conflicts, combating a pandemic – and perhaps also to an acute problem in your community or company. It is courageous to accept the situation as it is. Not because we think it's good, but because it is. Only when we acknowledge a situation and don't spend our energy on "talking nice and talking differently" do we gain the necessary strength for change.

Whether the outside world challenges us with complications or complexities – let's understand the varying fears we face in organizations and what we need in terms of leadership in these thrilling times.

Courage in the VUCA World

Rapid changes, uncertain outlooks, complex problems, and contradictory requirements characterize the VUCA world. The results of our actions are difficult to predict, and yesterday's truths may be obsolete tomorrow. Good dialog between experts and decision-makers is needed to find the right path. We need a good compass of purpose and values to guide our actions. We talk to those involved about this compass, the underlying facts, and options for action. And then we decide and act courageously – because we take risks with our actions.

Courage and Trust

Only when we see courage can we really begin to trust.

This might be familiar – a new boss or colleague joins the department or the company. The rumor mill rages, everyone talks about the person, and the question always comes up at some point.

"Can you trust them?" This is then usually checked using examples and stories about this person. And they are not trustworthy if it is said that they "hang their flag in the wind," "only has their personal interests in mind," and "has trouble making decisions." The person seems untrustworthy because they do not show courageous behavior, they step back from their promises and intentions when success is not the only possible outcome. If courageous behavior is nowhere to be seen, there is not going to be real trust. What you say is not enough; people will only develop real trust if you let your actions speak louder than your words through risk-taking behavior.

Trust is the goal of courageous leadership. Because trust is good for people and for their relationships, makes work more enjoyable, and leads to higher performance in teams and organizations. Paul J. Zak, author of the book *Trust Factor: The Science of Creating High-Performance Companies*, researched how a trustful working environment affects performance in companies. The results of his 2017 study are impressive. Employees in organizations with a high-trust culture report twice the level of energy, more commitment, higher productivity, and a greater willingness to stay than employees in companies with a low-trust culture. (Zak, 2017)

Real trust comes from reliability, even under adverse and high-risk circumstances. Only when others realize that you personally take on difficulties or disadvantages can material trust be built. That's why Anna only really began trusting me when we stood together against Daniel's accusations of having been misled by her market research analysis. She didn't expect that because it could have been detrimental for me to stand up to an influential boss in a corporate culture.

Oliver Kastalio, former CEO of WMF, had a similar experience. This is how he describes the importance of being a trusted leader:

> In this complex structure, you need authenticity, a strong connection between "brain and heart and gut," visible integrity of values and actions, the human must always remain distinguishable. Then you will be recognized as a positive figure of authority. And if you are authentic, you lead with courage. Because there are always situations in which the answer to complex challenges lies outside your comfort zone. Then you decide on a principle, or a value, or a specific goal and go into confrontation, accepting the risk.

When I started my job at my penultimate employer, I took over a management team of seasoned employees. Together, we developed an ambitious strategy with far-reaching goals. I knew that we had big plans and that they would only be achieved if these people – none of whom knew me – placed their full trust in me quickly. Trust was, on the one hand, based on professional competence and, on the other, on the personal integrity and reliability experienced by the employees. We are not impressed by integrity and reliability in "fair weather" but rather when someone takes risks in the face of pressure and difficult times and sticks to their principles, agreements, and promises. When I left the company after four years, we had achieved almost all our goals – two years earlier than I had thought possible. I had gained the trust of my team because they saw that I kept what I had agreed to, even when it was difficult – by rejecting additional projects, standing up for my employees, giving them freedom, contradicting my bosses, formulating ambitious goals, and winning over hesitant people with patience. The basis of all these interventions was, on the one hand, this clear strategy. It enabled us all to argue openly about the best solutions. On the other hand, I had personal convictions about how I wanted to lead the team and made these transparent from the jump so that everyone could measure and hold me up to them. I made myself "predictable" in a positive sense.

What creates trust? I asked this question in a workshop, and the result was as "banal" as it was moving. Banal, because all the thoughts we collected were actually "kindergarten pedagogy." You keep your promises. You don't claim someone else's work as your own. You don't speak ill of others. You help. You say something nice when someone does something well. You don't lie. You don't point the finger at others. You don't start rumors. And so on and so forth. As I said: kindergarten etiquette. It was moving that this list seemed very far removed from everyday working life for those present – and that in turn felt wrong. And it is: all these violations undermine trust in the organization. And a lack of trust in the workplace can cost you the health and performance of employees (Zak, 2017) as well as an organization's open communication and quick response time. Trust is the decisive factor in a high-performing organization – and it is created by leaders.

Courage and Morale

In my eyes, courageous leadership is also "moral leadership." I extend a heartfelt invitation to all the cynics, pragmatists, and disgruntled – courageous leadership is moral because its goal is human development and integrity. The egotistical pursuit of goals without regard for losses and moral norms may take you out of your comfort zone – and is therefore "courageous" – but is not at all what I would like to offer strength, tailwind, and support for with this book. Moral integrity is the guiding principle of courageous leadership, and I hope you will find suggestions and inspiration in this book to put it into practice in your own life.

Are there "moral imperatives" that we pursue in our courageous leadership? How do these present themselves? Currently, these are my answers:

Courageous leadership is respectful, appreciative, and offers cooperation "at eye level." Courageous leadership takes issue with acts of humiliation, discrimination, and socially destructive behavior, demands change, and imposes sanctions if change is not enacted sustainably. Whether this is a transfer, non-promotion, or dismissal depends on the circumstances. In voluntary contexts (NGOs, political parties, etc.), this is often protracted but must be tackled in the same way.

Time and again, people choose ethical behavior over the rules and norms of their organization or environment. The examples of Benno Dorer at Clorox (see page 109), a multi-billionaire entrepreneur calling against a vote for a far-right, racist party, or whistleblowers like Edward Snowden and Chelsea Manning are proof of this. That is virtuous and precious.

Saving the climate, the complete restructuring of our energy supply from "black" energy to green energy is urgent, the alternatives are deadlier and more expensive than procrastination. It will take major reshaping projects, consistency, and urgency to develop our economy into a more sustainable one. This is a task for every organization and every company – including every manager.

Encouraging leadership aims to strengthen justice. Whether in matters of diversity and inclusion, salary structures in the company or speaking time in political parties: justice is an important moral task for peaceful coexistence. It's a basic human need. Experiencing injustice is incredibly stressful and evokes negative feelings, especially anger and aggression. I know many managers who played with unfair behavior because they found it "funny" how unfairly treated people allow themselves to be tormented, lose their strength, and become defensive. Throughout my career, I have witnessed a lack of respect for humans in the workplace. It's simple yet we tend to leave our norms, that all people are born equal and with dignity, at the company door. Courageous leadership strives for fair systems, fair treatment, and negotiations at eye level.

Harder, Better, Faster, and Stronger?

More sales and earnings than last quarter, lower costs than three years ago, more efficient than the competition, increasing profitability for six quarters, and so on and so forth – PowerPoint presentations and annual reports are peppered with such success stories of key financial figures. The dividend for investors must be right, otherwise, the money will go where you get more bang for your buck. How can this continue? This system has brought immense wealth to very few, comfortable prosperity to many, and a life of poverty to even more. And it has brought us all the exploitation of Earth's natural resources and the destruction of the climate. The future of humanity is at risk, and the poorer the population and the individual are, the darker the collective and individual prospects for a good life become.

The transformation of our society, "in which nature and people are reconciled," needs all of us. This is how Göpel (2020, p. 183) describes this vision (translation by author): "A future in which all the big and small drivers, which instigate us to a way of life that today neither brings the greatest happiness for the greatest number nor allows the foundations of life, on which all our happiness depends, to regenerate, are pacified. A future in which we can better share again and have learned to be content with what is."

Saying goodbye to the financial "more, more, more" doctrine will take time, but we must start now. We can define "value creation" more broadly than in monetary input–output calculations – in social, cultural, and ecological values that processes, companies, or society at large produces. This transformation requires the courage of many and will not take place in a collective comfort zone. CO2-reduced mobility, massive reduction of waste, and circular economy make previous value chains obsolete and demand new behavior from all of us. This requires new concepts, a great deal of understanding, and different legislation, which we can ensure if we have the courage.

In the following chapters, I invite you to begin shaping organizations in such a way that common concerns and individual effectiveness come into a continuous creative and productive exchange. For great results, good work, and encouraging interaction.

Leadership, Courage, and Morale

If you want to make a difference, you need to create *trustful connections*. People achieve more, are more creative, and are healthier when they feel trust(ed). Working in unison with others is a source of pure joie de vivre. Courageous behavior that brings what is said and what is done into harmony creates trust.

Encouraging leadership follows a *moral compass* and makes its values transparent.

Our world needs a lot of courageous leadership for a climate-friendly, peaceful, just world – because it is "VUCA" and many of the challenges *cannot be tackled with old concepts*. Such a transformation requires the courage of many individuals who, where they can, step out of their comfort zone and *demand, offer, prepare, and enable new paths*. In view of the crises we have created, it is the task that calls us all.

References

Göpel, M. (2020). *Unsere Welt neu denken: Eine Einladung*. Ullstein Hardcover.

USAHEC. (2022, December 6). *Who first originated the term VUCA (Volatility, Uncertainty, Complexity and Ambiguity)? - USAHEC Find Your Answer*. Retrieved October 23, 2024, from https://usawc.libanswers.com/faq/84869

Zak, P. J. (2017, January–February). The neuroscience of trust. *Harvard Business Review*, 84–90. https://hbr.org/2017/01/the-neuroscience-of-trust

Chapter 9

Fear in Organizations

Here is my overview of fear in organizations, observed by my coachees or myself and collected in this chapter.

Fears Due to External Developments

As discussed, the "VUCA world" (volatile – uncertain – complex – ambiguous) causes anxiety in many: the unpredictability, the frequency (and number) of events, the extent of the changes, and the convolutedness of possible solutions stress us out.

Sales are shrinking and so are profits; you can't cut costs as quickly as the money goes missing. Because markets are shrinking and becoming obsolete due to new products (think of carriages, mechanical typewriters, corded telephones, cassette recorders, and so on). Or because a (new?) competitor is much more successful and "wipes" you off the market. Anxiety about jobs and promotion opportunities is rampant in the organization.

Turnover and profits are okay so far, but value creation is shifting massively, the *previous business model no longer works*, and internal restructuring follows, spreading fear and anxiety: job relocations abroad, digitalization, and automation of previous work steps – jobs are up for grabs and people are afraid of what might come next.

Legal adjustments and political developments require a massive change in processes. Where companies used to be able to operate relatively freely and as they saw fit, they now face existential penalties or the withdrawal of their business license. The climate crisis and our CO_2 reduction targets are forcing many companies to comprehensively restructure their entire value chain if they want to survive in the long term. This will not pay for itself out of petty cash, important skills may be missing, and nobody knows the complete solution. All approaches to date have been inadequate.

DOI: 10.4324/9781003582724-11

Internally Generated Fears

There is the *aggressive-despotic-intimidating* form of leadership that actively threatens people, demands outright obedience, tolerates no dissent, creates a lack of transparency, and is simply toxic. There is fear because it is actively and "publicly" induced through humiliation and punishment. Lacking or incomplete information is an additional source of insecurity.

There is *weak leadership* that allows ambiguity, contradictions, and confusion, but (at least) does not actively stir up fear. Silo mentality, competing projects, overwhelming demands, and fear of making mistakes are the consequence.

Toxic individuals stir up fear in their organization through intimidation, harassment, unfair behavior, and ridiculing colleagues and employees. This may or may not be a line manager. The behavior may go unaccounted for because there is no culture of trust and no whistleblowing system. Or it may be tolerated because the toxic person has made a name for themselves in the eyes of those in charge. Or the management is simply indifferent to the damage being done.

Collective burnout due to complete overload and exhaustion. Constant pressure, hardly or non-attainable goals, too little resources – the organization is poorly positioned (tasks vs. resources, demands vs. reality). There is hardly any sense of achievement. It is never enough. If something succeeds, the next unsolvable task is already waiting. The feeling of permanent failure and exhaustion deprives people of courage and strength, the experience of self-efficacy is missing.

The great diffusion of responsibility. When costly and consequential decisions are made in complicated organizations, the people in charge get scared. Everyone tries to hand over the decision to the next person, hide behind organizational charts, or put the decision on the back burner. The fear of making a serious misstep is greater than the energy required to solve the problem.

Just don't make any mistakes. In a culture of perfectionism, mistakes cause a big fuss, no matter how (ir)relevant they are. The head of finance sent the investment application for 7 million euros back to his colleague because he found two insubstantial typos in the internal documentation. The result is a delay of several days, for nothing. Work results are checked for errors as a matter of priority by superiors, and if they are found, a big scene is caused. Whoever made the mistake feels belittled, a failure, and inadequate.

"That's how we do it here. And not any other way!" Everyone involved in the system has their routine and familiar solutions. Suggestions for change generate resistance, lack of understanding and anger, as they are perceived as criticism and questioning of the status quo. The fear of the new is huge because people have stuck with the old for a very long time.

At the same time, many "tried and tested" and "familiar" things no longer work at all – we are in the VUCA world after all.

Rumors, hounding, and slander are spread, cultivated, and tolerated. People talk badly about others, damage their reputation, or spin real intrigues – the "house of cards." An incredible amount of energy goes into creating, spreading, and controlling these stories. The organization barely fulfills its core task, as too many are busy harming others or trying to prevent damage to themselves. Fear for their own reputation, their job, and their connection to colleagues is rampant.

Relationships, favors, and networks dominate everything. Sometimes it's a hierarchical system – those who belong to the boss's circle of friends make a career, lead high-profile projects, and earn more. It can also be a "clique system" in which separate groups or factions are at odds with each other and stand in competition with each other. There is a great fear of falling out of the successful network or group or getting beat by the "enemy" faction.

Unambitious comfort. Whether "work-to-rule," sluggish processing of orders or prolonged silence in team meetings. Fear of effort has sucked all the energy out of people, there is no joy in one's own impact, in creating, in good work, and in satisfying labor.

So much for my "pathology of organized fear" in companies and other large social structures, all of which I was "allowed" to experience. Obviously, they can also overlap and reinforce each other in the most dreadful way. Following the announcement of restructuring, I have always experienced an increase and intensification of my internal anxiety. The same applies if external events are not reflected upon, processed, and discussed with the workforce in a way that provides orientation. In the following chapters, I offer various "treatment options" that social systems can use to heal. And, once again, they require courageous behavior, stepping out of the fear-mongering dynamics.

Fears in Organizations

Fears in organizations can be triggered by *external or internal developments*. External developments deprive organizations of their business foundations. *Those who do not innovate, change, and adapt can pack their bags*. This can set off fears. There are also many internally triggered fears – by *despotic managers, opaqueness, deficient, uncooperative dealings*. External and internal developments often overlap and intensify the fears of those partaking in the system. Work on and within the system is then necessary to restore capacity and effectiveness.

Chapter 10

Compass of a Courageous Organization

In Chapter 9, I described fears widespread in organizations or companies. The phenomena of the VUCA world can exacerbate them further. What can be your first steps to get out of a fear cycle? I will first describe the "ideal picture" of a courageously led organization, in which courage does not need to consist of protecting against toxic behavior, but rather of pursuing the purpose of the organization, even if the path is not always visible, difficulties are encountered, or mistakes are made (there will always be mistakes).

In order for people in organizations to act courageously, i.e. to leave their comfort zone again and again and reach the growth zone, common foundations, and agreements are necessary. Courageous action is worthwhile since the ever-changing environment in which organizations operate and therein change themselves perpetually demands new ways of thinking, acting, and reacting. Nothing stays the same.

Having a compass allows everyone to have a clear reference for individual and joint action:

1 Why we do what we do: The purpose of the organization is clarified, a vision of success is agreed on
2 How we work: Values that guide action as well as a management style are formulated and – above all – practiced. A system of rules ("governance") describes responsibilities, tasks, rights, and duties. The clear distribution of tasks and decision-making channels limit arbitrariness and personal advantage
3 Develop a strategy: How do we want to pursue our purpose in the medium term? What do we do, what do we not do, and what do we need? All these questions can be answered by a proper strategy

These three fundamentals – purpose with an image of success, guidelines for action, and strategy – are the bases for trustful collaboration.

DOI: 10.4324/9781003582724-12

Establishing the Basics: Why, What, and How?

"What is our purpose, what do we want to achieve, how do we want to work together, what is our strategy, what does everyone want to achieve?" If all members of a team have the same or matching answers to these questions, then this is a great prerequisite for a courageous environment – where clarity, commitment, and collaboration live.

Table 10.1 Compass for the Courageous Organization

The compass: conversations and outcomes

Step	*Conversation about*	*Outcome*
1	Why are we here?	Common purpose
2	What is our picture of success? What do we aim for?	Pull instead of pressure as the driver of action
3	What values guide us? What is our governance? Who has what role, what responsibility? How do we make things happening among us?	Smooth ways of working
4	What are our measures of success? What do we know about the world, our capabilities, our resources? What do we do to achieve our goals? What do we choose to not do?	A strategy that guides all major choices
5	How are we progressing? What is in the way? How can we support each other?	Executing the strategy, moving towards picture of success
6	What have we learned? How do we celebrate success? What is next?	Celebrating success, learning, and getting ready for the next frontier of impact.

These basics create the arc that goes from ambition, through guiding ideas for collaboration, to strategy and activities – an arc that my company name "ambitionize" describes as well: from purpose to action.

You can develop such a compass "anytime and anywhere" and it is particularly important when conflicts are piling up in a team or organization, and there is little interaction or positive energy. "Always" also means "again and again" – in our dynamic world, you constantly tap the compass for its validity and functionality, offer debate, explain ideas to new participants and invite feedback (Table 10.1).

"Collective Crossing of the Heart": Purpose, Mission, and the Like

Purpose is the guiding star for an organization, a company, a team, and the answer to the question "Why are we here?". The answer comes more from the heart than from pure rational thought. In order to mobilize all our energy, we need a purpose that touches and mobilizes us personally. In some teams, this conversation is intensive and short, but in most cases, it takes some time to understand each other and to formulate a coherent purpose for everyone. The aim should be to formulate the purpose of the organization in one to three sentences. You should also be clear about the purpose of temporary projects. Here are a few examples of "purpose sentences" or missions:

> We create high-performance organizations in which people enjoy their work. The burst of energy, the outstanding results and the team spirit that emerge are our driving force. At ambitionize we strengthen courage, so together we can create better work for a better world.
>
> (ambitionize, 2020)

> We will provide branded products and services of superior quality and value that improve the lives of the world's consumers, now and for generations to come. As a result, consumers will reward us with leadership sales, profit and value creation, allowing our people, our shareholders and the communities in which we live and work to prosper.
>
> (P&G, 2023)

> Greenpeace is a global network of independent campaigning organizations that use peaceful protest and creative confrontation to expose global environmental problems and promote solutions that are essential to a green, just, and joyful future.
>
> (Greenpeace USA, 2023)

In countless workshops, teams have worked with me to develop the purpose of their company, their business unit, or an important project. In between, there is always some tedious juggling of words, and at the end, when the common articulation has been found, a new energy, curiosity, and drive emerges. Once the purpose has been found, everyone can boldly ask at any time during further collaboration: "Is this consistent with our agreed purpose?" And that helps everyone to focus and make decisions purposefully.

Painting the Success Story

Götz Werner, the former head of the drugstore chain "dm," explains the difference between fear-based and encouraging leadership in an interview:

> In life, you don't need pressure, you need pull. If you want to fly, you need thermals. Airplanes fly because pull is created. I myself am the father of seven children - they all only respond to pull. Customers, who buy from us come because they feel a pull, not because someone is kicking them in the butt. From a philosophical point of view, the pressure thing is a fallacy invented by the devil.
>
> (Translation by the author) (Kainrath, 2017)

> We are really successful. We've grown by around 10% every year for the last 10 years, and everything is going swell. Now we must consider whether we should develop this new business area further. It's very promising. There's a huge amount of revenue coming our way, which will only be possible with a transformation of the company – in terms of quality management, processes, and quantities. But we don't have to do that because we can continue to grow as before without this business area.

This is how Pete*, Managing Director of a medium-sized technology company, identified its need for strategy development. Eight weeks later, shareholders approved a strategy that seeks to double revenue within five years. Since then – that was in the summer of 2018 – the company has been growing despite many obstacles, occasional failures, and delays that go with it.

In order to mobilize energy sustainably, you need a concrete, tangible image of the future – similar to the visualization exercise I presented in the first part of the book. At the beginning of this process, "anything goes" – you want to have as rich, stimulating, and complete an understanding of everyone's ideas as possible. Maybe you're not sure about the time frame for the vision of success – are we talking 12 months, 3, or maybe even 10 years? This is an important orientation. Once the ideas have been collected and understood, you start talking about commonalities, contradictions, and tensions. Then, you can sort, prioritize, and decide. The results can be recorded in pictures, texts, and figures.

Pete's team settled on the picture "from workshop to industrial player." With this picture in mind, choices about revenue targets, key clients, and adaptations of the whole value chain became much clearer.

In such discussions, we usually learn that there are very different ideas about "success" in a team. They arise from different perspectives, skills, and goals, as well as from past experiences or frustrations. Here, too, I implore you to be courageous: address the contradictions and tensions and look for a common solution. In my experience, 90% of tensions can be resolved through carefully listening and properly understanding the situation and people involved.

The last 10%, if you're into harmony and consensus, require you to step out further of your comfort zone: these are issues that require a decision, and no matter what you decide, someone in your team, one of your customers, a colleague, may not be happy with you. Sometimes, it's like that. Listen to dissatisfaction, explain your decision, invite acceptance, and take the next step.

The "How": Values, Guidelines, and Governance

Benno Dorer is CEO of the Clorox Company, a US-based billion-dollar company, as the coronavirus pandemic rages in April 2020. The consumption of disinfectants quintupled in some market segments. It was impossible to meet demand in full. What to do? Serve the most profitable market segments? Prioritize strategic customers? What is the right thing to do? Benno and his management team were guided by the company's purpose ("we champion people to be well and thrive every single day") and the company value "do the right thing." This value is clearly defined: "We lead with integrity, and we earn trust – in every moment and with every decision. We are hungry to grow our business and believe that winning only counts if it's done the right way" (The Clorox Company, 2021).

Ultimately, company management decided to prioritize hospitals and care facilities. Because that is where lives were being saved. This decision had serious consequences for Clorox – many customers could not be supplied, competitors filled the gaps, and consumers complained. The company earned less money than it would have with a different approach. And yet the company stuck to its decision, which was in line with the company's purpose, values, and principles.

The impact of such an approach is high: employees see and feel that purpose and values really do guide action and are not only applied when it is easiest to do so. This encourages open and courageous conversations for the right path. Values that guide actions and tip the scales in decisions are an important aspect of the "how" and create clear references for courageous behavior – insofar as they are lived, and one can openly explore how best to act on these values.

Another important aspect to avoid arbitrariness, confusion, and friction is good governance, preferably in written form and accessible to everyone in the organization. Since 2021, there has even been an International Organization for Standardization (ISO) norm for this. The ISO norm 37000 describes "...

Good governance as a people-based system through which an organization is directed, supervised, and held accountable for achieving its defined purpose in an ethical and responsible manner." (Lingscheid, 2022)

Whether you focus on the guiding values in a team or an organization, develop an entire governance system, or formulate management guidelines – there are many ways to create a binding framework that benefits everyone involved. Depending on the size of the organization, its legal definition, applicable certifications and licenses, there are also mandatory elements of governance that need to be written down. You can formulate a "manifesto" that can be used regularly in meetings, bring new colleagues on board, or review difficult decisions:

Take this manifesto to your team – what suits you, what do you formulate differently, and how can such a manifesto serve you?

Manifesto of the Courageous Organization

To fulfill the purpose of our organization, we want to be courageous: try new things, be creative, take risks, improve, contribute, and achieve more.

Everyone wants to have a positive impact, do excellent work, and successfully pursue our common purpose.

We create transparency: about purpose, strategies, plans, and achievements as well as about the roles and tasks of the players.

We work together: all goals in the organization complement each other and build on each other. Conflicts are a task, not a problem.

Leadership shows perspectives for joint contribution and success as well as for individual growth.

We decide, we lead. Decisions are implemented and we are curious about what works and what does not. We adapt.

Our environment is constantly changing. We stay curious, continuously reviewing opportunities and risks, as well as the impact of our actions. We keep moving.

We agree on and regularly review organizational principles guiding our decisions and actions.

Develop and Implement Strategy

A strategy frames the way in which the purpose is to be fulfilled, how you will achieve your vision of success. You choose what you do and what you don't, which resources are available for what, which projects are tackled, in which order, etc. There are countless strategy tools you can choose from.

When developing a strategy, I pay particular attention to the following:

1 The purpose of giving your organization direction
2 Agreement on a common image of success
3 There is a thorough analysis of external and internal influences, opportunities, and resources
4 All resulting options have been seen, evaluated, and decided
5 Overall targets and interim targets are set
6 The main actions for reaching your targets are described
7 Responsibilities are clear
8 Everyone involved knows and understands the strategy
9 A feedback loop is built in so that progress can be identified and corrected if necessary
10 The curiosity, energy, and creativity of all those involved are brought to bear, and (maybe surprising) solutions are found in intensive debates

A strategy developed in this way provides energy, clarity, and a focus on results, which in turn enables courageous action and courageous discussions: many options ought to be considered when developing a strategy. Do we want to grow with product innovations? Or through geographic expansion? Can we activate more sales channels? Do we do all three? Once the decisions have been made, those responsible can implement the strategy with all their might, budgets are made available, suitable personnel is found, and so on. Even if the strategy takes you out of your previous comfort zone – management's strategy will give you support and strength for implementation, even if you are entering unfamiliar territory.

"Why don't you take a look at this prototype from Wizardy," my managing director suggests. "Great idea, quite useful, it'll be a bestseller, you should add it to your project portfolio!" One look at the prototype makes it clear to me: I'm looking at a great product that doesn't fit the strategy of my team. We need products to strengthen our coffee or waste disposal brands. We don't have a brand for "little household helpers" and we can't build another brand. We are looking for sales in food retail, not in owner-managed specialist stores. And it is becoming increasingly clear: the managing directors know each other well and that plays a role in evaluating their "great ideas." Good idea or not, we are not able to include this sort of prototype in our portfolio. We have a clearly formulated strategy, and this product doesn't tick a single of its boxes. The clarifying discussion with the managing director is exhausting and tense, but in the end, the strategic understanding of everyone involved prevails and we have the courage to say "no." Me to the managing director and the managing director to his buddy.

We did this successfully since the need for improvement and dissatisfaction do not stem from personal sensitivities but can be discussed in relation to a strategy and its implementation. And because the development of the strategy – getting to the bottom of issues, perspectives, and tensions – has led to a deeper mutual understanding making it easier to discuss difficult topics.

Goals for Everyone

> All managing directors are realizing that the sales manager is simply not asserting himself. We won't reach our targets that way. I look stupid because the digital product I developed is not successful on the market, but I can't do anything because sales is not my area of expertise! How can I give the sales manager feedback or resolve the situation another way?

This is how my coachee, a brand manager, complains about a goal being out of reach because someone else is not doing their job. He sees a few options, but none of them feel adequate. Until I ask how focused the sales department is on making this product a success. And then it becomes clear: not at all. Sales are mired in contradictory and irreconcilable expectations. In a complicated matrix organization, everyone communicates their goals to the sales department and there is no real understanding of how individual employees should do everything expected of them. Then you need to factor in that a new digital product will cost the salesperson orders in the medium term – and a strategically central project can turn into a disaster quickly. Once he has realized what's wrong, my coachee chooses a truly courageous undertaking: get everyone involved around a table, and set goals in such a way that the sales team has an honest chance of implementing them.

If you or your organization are slow to boldly implement your strategy: check whether the target systems and reward mechanisms and the strategy really fit together and can also be implemented by "the last person in the chain." Regardless of which management tool you work with, whether "agile" or with key performance indicators (KPIs) – if the targets and reward systems of individuals are in conflict, you have already built in a courage curtailer.

The Compass and the VUCA World

Purpose, values and guidelines, strategies – is this even worthwhile in a VUCA world? When energy prices explode, supply chains collapse, war breaks out, what remains?

Here is a guide to the validity period of the various elements of the organizational compass shared (Table 10.2).

Table 10.2 Timetable for the Courageous Organization

Time scope of main elements of an organizational compass

	Short (>1 year)	*Medium (2–5 years)*	*Long (over 5 years)*
Purpose of the organization			X
Values			X
Management guidelines			X
Structure of the Organization		X	
Description of core processes		X	
Decision matrix		X	
Picture of success		X	X
Analyses	X	X	
Strategic options		X	
Qualitative goals		X	
Strategic measures	X	X	
Quantitative targets (OKR, KPI, etc.)	X		
Operational planning	X	X	

This overview can help you understand the cycle of the essential conversations and work processes to keep your compass relevant and up to date.

Compass for the Courageous Organization

Agreement on the purpose, the vision of success, a management mission statement, responsibilities, and strategy creates orientation and commitment for all those involved. Differences of opinion and perspective can be easily negotiated because the *basis for cooperation* is clear. The risk of personal arbitrariness and selfish pursuit of interests is reduced – because everyone can – and must – explain themselves in relation to the compass. This *promotes individual and collective courage*, as you can concentrate on the task of the organization.

References

ambitionize. (2020). *ambitionize® consulting, training and coaching*. Retrieved October 23, 2024, from https://ambitionize.com/

Greenpeace USA. (2023, September 11). *About - Greenpeace USA*. Greenpeace USA - We Fight for a Greener, More Peaceful World. Retrieved October 23, 2024, from https://www.greenpeace.org/usa/about/

Kainrath, V. (2017, January 21). Grundeinkommen stellt Gesellschaft vom Kopf auf die Füße. *Der Standard*. Retrieved October 23, 2024, from https://www.derstandard.at/story/2000051252761/goetz-werner-alte-s-stellt-eine-ganze-gesellschaft-vom-kopf

Lingscheid, U. (2022, April 27). *ISO 37000:2021 – Good Governance - QM-aktuell.de*. QM-aktuell.de. Retrieved October 23, 2024, from https://www.qm-aktuell.de/iso-370002021-good-governance/

P&G. (2023, August 16). *P&G purpose, values and principles*. Procter & Gamble. Retrieved October 23, 2024, from https://us.pg.com/policies-and-practices/purpose-values-and-principles/

The Clorox Company. (2021, July). *Purpose & values*. Retrieved October 23, 2024, from https://www.thecloroxcompany.com/company/purpose-values/

Chapter 11

Courage Tools for Many

Whether in a management team, a project group, or a board of directors – which tools increase your collective courage, your continuous ability, and your willingness to leave your comfort zone and seek out new things? Just try it. Maybe courageous behavior will eventually become your core competence.

Create Commitment

I've been standing in front of the whiteboard for 15 minutes with the same question, asking it for the fifth time: "How often do you want to meet as a management team?" We have already had a day and a half of intensive crisis consultation – the business unit of a large corporation is in the red, one of their plants is losing millions every month and the newly assembled management team, spread around the world, is looking for a way out of this mess. We discuss the way forward and I simply don't get an answer to my question. Everyone says something without giving me a tangible answer. So, for the sixth time, I ask: "How often do you want to meet in your management team?" Once more, excuses and no clear answer. Finally, I offer a new question:

> What is happening here? The list of measures you have drawn up says "regular management team meetings." I've been standing here for fifteen minutes now trying to get an answer from you to this very simple question of implementation. While your house is burning, such simple things are keeping you from getting the fire hose. What's going on?

First, a great deal of embarrassment. Then a jolt of "This isn't working. We can't spend this long on something trivial like this." My coachees realize that they have been looking for excuses and problems instead of simple answers. A few minutes later, an agreement is reached, and in the arrangements that follow we have commitment, solutions, and pragmatism for

DOI: 10.4324/9781003582724-13

simple issues. I then spoke to the managing director – those last 15 minutes were also very enlightening for him. He tends to lead with restraint, trusts in his team, and believes that the right results will be achieved even without his interventions. Now he has seen that sometimes his energy is required to achieve results faster and he decides to challenge his team more to work at a faster pace and with a solution-oriented approach.

I often encounter the nirvana of non-commitment in my work with organizations. Teams with an infinite number of "would've, could've, should've" and in their workshops, flipchart after flipchart is filled with measures. Until the peculiar moment in which I ask "who?" and "by when?" and suddenly all energy and motivation vanished. We then reflect on this – how do lists of unfinished activities come about, what do we hope for if there is no name next to a measure, and so on. Here, honesty is key. That's how we work our way out of the hole — by respecting resources, setting priorities, and making commitments that can be honored. For many, the first time takes courage – for example, when someone in the team says what they can no longer accomplish, or which project might have to be delayed.

In countless organizations, commitment is outside people's comfort zone. There is a culture of unaccountability. Commitment tends to frighten rather than energize. Yet commitment and reliability are an elementary component of (building) trust, which is why I put emphasis on this learning step for teams. If a team is not used to openly discussing expectations, goals, and the limits of what is possible, this is an important step of courage. Creating commitment then becomes very simple: who does what and by when? Done. As we have experienced, these simple questions can get stuck in a thick sludge of resistance, excessive demands, and evasion. But you can shovel them out of the way with patience and perseverance.

We or Me?

Then there is a usually small, sometimes large hurdle on the track to courageous commitment. The "who?" becomes a "we"! What initially sounds nice and collegial can quickly turn out to be a double-edged sword – perhaps even an unpredictable morning star. To enable honest discussions about resources and binding agreements, I invite team members to name a single person with the final responsibility. This does not mean that you do everything on your own. It means ensuring that the desired result is achieved. In the vast majority of cases, this is not possible alone, and you also talk about the additional work, support requirements, etc. However, this does not change that one person should raise their hand to take responsibility for the result.

Why is this so important? One person can take responsibility, knows what they can do, and who can (or must) help where. **Individual responsibility brings clarity.**

"When I die, I want the people I did group projects with to lower me into my grave, so they can let me down one last time." If several people are responsible, things can turn out unfairly quick. The "hard-working," responsible person shoulders most of the burden, while others only do the bare minimum. When the project is successfully delivered, everyone comes back and claims their share of the glory – after all, they were responsible, weren't they? **Individual responsibility brings fairness.**

The nebulous responsibility requires constant coordination, follow-up, and clarification, which does not bring the result any closer. **Individual responsibility is efficient.**

Results over Cliques

Do you still remember the story of my conflict with Daniel? Back then, my motivation for backing Anna was my conviction that my team can only make the necessary contribution if we work with the available facts "regardless of the person," draw analytically correct conclusions, and are not persuaded by internal political interests. That was not heroic, but my promise to the company: "Facts over opinion." That's why I didn't hesitate to boldly leave my comfort zone and stand up to Daniel.

If personal success in an organization does not depend on whether someone pursues the common purpose and delivers the necessary results, courageous behavior becomes difficult. Then it's more about "who knows and likes who," mutual favors, and internal alliances, as I described in "Pathologies of Fear": Opinions win out over facts, managing or fighting over personal relationships dominate and the focus is not on performance but on the interests of individuals. In such an organization, there is little courage to serve a common purpose and a great deal of willingness to align oneself with the (most) powerful. You cannot change such a culture from one day to the next. Cultural change in a company takes, in my experience, at least seven years – even longer in very large organizations. But if you don't start, nothing will ever change. What could be a crucial step in such cultural change? It is to implement a system of transparent and measurable performance evaluation, which will be decisive for individual advancement in the organization, and that all members of the organization agree to. This is the prerequisite for removing both positive and negative bias from personnel development, curbing nebulous cliques, and creating a transparent platform for collaboration – and courageous behavior. You can start this in your direct environment and formulate clear expectations and performance criteria in and with your team. Be aware that the whole organization might not work this way and that other managers might use different criteria than you do. The limits that you and your team will encounter should be taken with composure and patience.

Omit Labels and Judgments

Françoise* pondered for a long time, then carefully crept her way toward criticizing my leadership behavior. She explained to me, somewhat nervously but very matter-of-factly, that I simply talked too much in our management team meetings. By rehashing the same idea and re-presenting it in newer and more detailed ways. Understandably, my team found this extremely annoying. I hadn't realized this – a blind spot! I thought my team had been hanging on my lips in admiration, but all they did was suppress a yawn. At the same time, I was glad that Françoise had pointed this out. I thanked her accordingly and felt her relief. In the following meetings, I changed my behavior, asking whether I had talked enough, and we even joked about my excessive talking. Consequently, our meetings became more efficient. Word got around in my team about what had happened between Françoise and me, and my people were increasingly open in making suggestions for other improvements, even some that were difficult for me personally. Our team got better and better as a result – more open, more reflective, and also happier because we could talk about a lot of things. That's how a tiny bit of courage builds more courage, courage then builds trust, and that's how we impact our collaborations.

I'm sure Françoise* had thought long and hard about how she could make me see the effect of my communication behavior. "She's so vain and conceited, likes to hear herself talk..." and many other judgments one could imagine. How would I have reacted if Françoise had come to me with one of these labels? Hopefully, I would have concentrated on her courage and the facts described, but perhaps I would have felt angry, attacked, and misunderstood and found Françoise disrespectful. What can you do when told, "You seem to like hearing yourself talk"? If we walk around with such judgments about others and then find the "courage" to unload them, nothing good comes of it. The reaction then depends on the distribution of power (hurt and humiliated when the boss does it, indignant and dismissive when the employee dares to). Judgments create distance, weaken mutual trust, and block change.

What do you do if an employee comes to you with harsh criticism or unpleasant judgment? They want to address a grievance they have experienced. With them, find out what exactly they observed, what needs have been violated, and help them to communicate more progressively and find a good solution. This will increase their impact, self-reflection will make them stronger, and the empathy experienced will make them feel like a valued colleague. You can also invite similar conversations in team meetings to avoid harsh judgments among your team. Since we all can't always be wise, here is a nice outlet:

"Recreational Bitching"

After a few hours with my management team, our team coach Sarah, visibly upset, blurts out:

> Are you really so sure that it's everyone else not doing a good job, that you're the ones having been spoon-fed with wisdom? What's happening that you're constantly talking about "us" and "them" – aren't you all in the same company?

Abashed and sheepish silence from all of us. We had fallen for the lure of judgment and distancing ourselves. The reasons are irrelevant now, but, at the core, we had become self-righteous and fallen into a somewhat self-important victim role. Sarah had recognized this without fault. And then a very special energy arose. We agreed to make real changes. We would no longer talk about "us versus them." We would no longer talk about dramas but instead about opportunities and what to do next. And then we gave ourselves a little "present": in every meeting, we were allowed to spend a total of five minutes on "recreational bitching." Five minutes in which we indulge in childish and immature drama. No longer than five minutes, but that was enough.

This agreement completely changed the mood of our meetings. We had more energy, found better solutions, and the relationship with other departments also improved. Because we showed respect and appreciation for others, our reputation increased for the better. One particular result of this positive image of the management team was that more and more people from other departments wanted to join. They saw we had a good atmosphere and that we delivered exciting projects, and they wanted to be part of this story.

Courage Tools for Many

Mutual trust increases with commitment and reliability. Clarity in individual responsibilities helps everyone to "do their thing" instead of waiting in a vague hope for others. The more you agree on comprehensible and meaningful goals, the achievement of which is also rewarded, the weaker cliques, favoritism, and intrigues for personal gain become. By not judging and condemning others, but focusing on opportunities for development, everyone can learn better and pursue a common purpose.

Chapter 12

Leading People to Courage

Clarity of purpose, vision of success, strategy, and responsibilities – these are the best conditions that a manager or management team can create to promote courageous behavior. In other words, behavior through which as many people as possible dare to step out of their comfort zone if this is necessary to achieve a purpose or goal.

Inviting Courage in a Team

> The key to the courage room door is an attitude on the part of the boss that invites everyone to give their best. And in our complex world, there are sometimes debates and differing opinions, and you can't come up with the best solutions without discussing them openly. So, there is a boss who not only puts up with it, but also invites critical and different perspectives.

This is how Oliver Kastalio describes his experience of courageous leadership.

The more you adopt a curious, open, and inviting attitude toward the demands, tasks, and adversities coming your way, the more courageous conversations can be had. You ask questions that do not feed fears, but signal confidence, connection, and openness. Especially in organizations that are hierarchical, error-oriented, and simply slow, you can encourage more people to participate with the words you choose.

These questions can be just as natural as questions about budget, resources, or risks. By asking them, you allow yourself and your team to step out of your comfort zones and gain a fresh perspective. You can then evaluate the exciting answers together and give the bold options a fair chance.

DOI: 10.4324/9781003582724-14

Questions for More Courage

"What would we do, if we weren't afraid?"

"What is the bravest (riskiest) thing we could do?"

"What opportunities are there right now? Are there any arising from the difficulties?"

"What we are planning here is uncharted territory. Nobody knows for certain what is right and what is wrong. We will make mistakes. That's okay. We will do a lot of things right. Even better. Let's find out."

"What assumptions are we making here? What else could apply? Have we overlooked anything?"

"What is particularly difficult or stressful here now?"

"The situation is confusing, there are few certainties and way more uncertainties. How do we want to deal with this? What steps can we take?"

"Thank you for sharing this point of view. It's important to hear everybody out! Do you feel listened to?"

Maybe not everyone is in the mood, or some get annoyed by the questions and subsequent conversation. You can concentrate on those who join you in challenging the status quo. Those not involved may want to stay in their comfort zone, worry about their routine, or be annoyed by your "fantasies." So be it. You can also hold a meeting only with those who want to get out of their comfort zone. They allow all the energy to flow, and then, once you've let off steam, evaluate it again in a cool-collected way. Then, the non-participants can be an excellent first test of viability for your idea and the persuasiveness of your arguments. You can use them to find weaknesses in the proposal and improve it. Or the doubters have clever arguments, uncovered your "blind spot" and saved you from a big bluster.

Empowering Individuals

The product launch was dragging its feet in the first market we went for. The initiative was one of the first by the new global Chief Marketing Officer Terrence*, who wanted to prove how quickly a new brand and product can win in a market. As long as you are as assertive and brilliant a marketer as he is. Well, it didn't work. Millions of euros had been invested, and sales figures were going at a snail's pace -- far below expectations. The national company, which had launched the product and bore a large part of the costs, was dissatisfied and blamed Terrence's team poor concept and campaign. Terrence was convinced that the national company did a poor job and was more at fault than him. I had been hired by Terrence a few months earlier as the head of global market research and it was now my department's mission to find the "wrongdoer."

Claudio* had just joined my team. Super-smart, a great communicator, quick wits – just the right person for a "politically" sensitive task like this. When I made him the offer to take on the case, he declined at first, which, once again, spoke for his intelligence. There were fears as to whether he would be able to familiarize himself with the facts quickly and precisely enough as a newbie in the company. Also, how he could get to the bottom of this matter without ending up being resented by the relevant parties in the long term.

We discussed these legitimate concerns and agreed on some safeguards. He would work out the facts, get the data, and then we would work together on the analysis and conclusion regarding said facts together. I assured him that I trusted him with the analysis and that we would discuss all the results and interpretations so thoroughly that I could always jump in to support what he might (need to) say. And I promised that I would discuss conclusions and procedures with Terrence in such a way that Claudio would not suffer any injuries for doing a good job. Thank God, we had discussed everything in such detail – in our analysis, we discovered major flaws on the side of the head office as well as weaknesses in the local implementation. No one was left unscathed; Terrence was just able to blame some of it on the marketing director who had designed the launch. He also chalked it up to a rookie mistake and already had his eyes on much bigger and more important projects. Claudio overcame his "trial-by-fire" and positioned himself as a clever analyst and a trustworthy sounding board.

"Has anyone else ever shown courage on your behalf? What effect did that have on you?" Two questions I ask many interviewees. Here are three quotes from my interviews. The first is from Maira:

> Yes, when I worked for the UN in Afghanistan. I was lucky enough to have two incredibly courageous bosses. As a very young woman, they gave me an incredible amount of responsibility and said: "We trust you to do this." And then they really let me do it. This basic trust was great. They saw me as a person and empowered me. That gave me an incredible amount of strength.

Then one from Markus, who was Managing Director at Accenture and works as a political and cultural consultant: "My great mentor, who always trusted me to do more than I did myself. He always set the bar higher than I thought possible. That makes me happy to this day." Or

Anja, a fellow coach who does climbing as a competitive sport (we're talking about courage, after all):

> My colleague. He gave me a bunch of freelance jobs on behalf of his company that I wouldn't have dared to do myself. His leaps of faith enabled me to do so much more than I thought possible - and my own professional courage grew substantially.

Whether the respective bosses saw this as a leap of faith or simply had a clear view of my interviewee's capabilities: The effect of handing over responsibility is immense every time.

As a leader, you can play a crucial role in inspiring people in your team to act courageously. For example, by handing over tasks and responsibilities that take someone out of their comfort zone. Maybe you feel like just saying "You can do it!" or "I'll look after you!" is not enough. Then, you can actively lead someone out of the fear zone through the five steps of the courage zone. This can take place in a focused conversation if the fear relates to a very specific task or situation. Big career moves, changing location, taking on an important project – you may need more conversations to assist them successfully.

1 Perceiving fear: What does the fear consist of? Be precise, multi-layered answers are possible. Perceive all its aspects.
2 Cross your heart: What could be a good reason to overcome this fear? What sucks you out of the fear zone and propels you into the courage zone?
3 Perceiving realities: What can really go wrong? Is that likely? What can be done to minimize risk? What would success be – and what would it mean? What strengths can the person rely on? What weaknesses need to be considered? Who might be able to help?
4 Decide: What is your employee ready to do? What do they want to do? The decision can also be to practice something specific or to only take on a subtask first. Supporting measures and safety nets can be arranged.
5 Dare: Discuss when this bold step will be taken. And reconfirm what role you will play. Once the courageous step has been taken, evaluate what worked well, what still poses problems, and what ought to be done next. From a "meta-talk" about finding courage, your employees can learn how they'll want to act the next time they feel anxiety or fear.

"No one is born a master." When fear rages around you screaming "I can't do this, I don't have the skills," then practice is the answer. Only through repetition does a new skill become familiar and effortless. No consistent top-level performance is based solely on talent, improvisation, or nonchalance. Practicing, concentrating, and more practicing will make us master new skills in the long term, a reward for (y)our courage. Pointing to "talent" is not encouraging. Talent makes things easier, but it is not enough to achieve sustainable performance. You won't find any athletes or musicians who are first-class solely because of their talent. It's only because with their talent they practice, practice, and practice every day and regularly call on their skills in high-performance situations.

Please, Step Aside

For two years, Irene* has overseen the most expensive, large, and complicated project in my department: the global launch of an app that allows authorized personnel to view reports and analyses of market surveys at any time, any place. A significant milestone for us, which, after 24 months, we reached on schedule thanks to Irene mastering the subject, keeping people on board, and working incredibly hard. Now, the big moment is right around the corner – the app is to be presented to our CEO. For the first time ever, he will have direct access to the reports showing the performance of national market teams.

My boss will be there, I'm supposed to join, and, of course, Irene. I imagine the scenario: the CEO with three people dancing around him, despite only one person being important – Irene. We only have 20 minutes with the CEO, and the topic is quite challenging to explain. I only go to meetings like this if I have something to say that nobody else does. I know how much of a chatterbox my boss can be and how much time Irene will need to convey the essentials to our CEO. So, I decided to not go. I want to give Irene as much "airtime" as possible. It's her project. I'll get some spotlight another time. Simply stepping aside, and giving the other person space, shows faith and brings about courage.

Promoting the Brave

> She really fought for her convictions, that was obvious. It didn't make her very popular, she knew that, but she didn't care because the undertaking was more important to her. First, I saw her courage, and then I saw her as a top talent and backed her up.

This is how one CEO described how he promoted courage in his organization in our interview. He recognized "courage" as competence and made a corresponding personnel policy. You don't need to be a CEO to do this. When you have individuals reporting to you, you can make "shows courage" and "takes risks" a performance indicator and give the people showing such behavior more responsibility. I've already talked about how brave people sometimes stand alone. You can stand with them. Choose the right moment to offer conversation, and the courage to reflect on what was good and what wasn't. Offer fresh perspective.

In a five-day management seminar I was attending, the trainers set out to teach the forty or so participants organizational awareness and confront their individual limitations in leadership behaviors. I was more of a "participating observer" – I was six months pregnant, and I had no intention to get overly stressed. As the training progressed, I found the methods and attitude of the trainers increasingly questionable. There were a lot of demands, provocations, pressure, as well as irritating and unsettling interventions. The atmosphere became tense and aggressive, with individuals repeatedly trying to stand out with suggestions and tell everyone else what to do next. Nothing worked, the atmosphere turned sour. Then Kai* made his appearance: "We shouldn't go on like this. We're all doing it wrong..." Before he could continue, he is laughed and shouted at, and all the boiled-up frustration is poured over him. He is made the scapegoat. The trainers didn't intervene and let things take their course. At some point, everyone pulled themselves together as if their collective rejection of Kai's suggestions flipped a switch. And Kai? He was absolutely devastated. I sat next to him, and we talked. Reflecting on what had just happened. I listened and offered him my perspective – that I didn't think it had much to do with him, but that everyone was longing for a scapegoat, and it ended up being him. He just got a mouthful from a group of stressed and frustrated people, and I didn't want to see him isolated and alone because of his courage.

Overcome Pedantry

"That word has to be written without an apostrophe before the 's', you mean the plural, don't you?" This is not being pointed out by my English teacher, but rather the first comment I received on the strategy of my international market research department, which I am currently presenting to my colleague from finance, Eric*. Like me, he is in the second management level of an international 20-billion-euro company. I want to discuss how we can set up "Consumer & Market Intelligence" in a way that allows us to innovate faster, make better use of our brands, and find additional opportunities for revenue across the globe.

In my opinion, he is a vital strategic partner for anchoring "facts over opinions" as an attitude in senior management. And then this: "The apostrophe is in the wrong place." I cringe internally, annoyed for a millisecond about having misplaced the apostrophe, agree with him, and lead him back to a conversation about strategy rather than grammar. The rest of the meeting confirms my impression: he wasn't particularly interested in our work, didn't formulate any common interests and was mainly looking for flaws in our strategy and other points of "criticism" – like the apostrophe. I still don't know whether he behaved this way on the instructions of his boss (his and my boss couldn't stand each other), couldn't help himself or just wanted to act like I was inferior. The result was that I focused on "flawlessness" in the collaboration instead of the important, axis of market research and finance department for fact-based decisions.

Many managers have little tolerance for mistakes and were promoted into their roles because they made fewer mistakes than others. This makes them faster, more efficient, and "better" – an important factor for promotions in many professions, specialist areas, and industries. A boss focused on finding and correcting mistakes may sap energy, joy, and purpose from your work.

If you as a manager view your main task to be discovering, criticizing, and correcting mistakes, you are not a "manager." You're a ticket inspector. Leadership creates orientation, mobilizes resources, and ensures development. Finding and eliminating mistakes is a task, not the purpose of leadership. Of course, it's good not to make mistakes. It saves resources and ensures quality. However, there are tasks that can only be tackled – and completed – if you have the courage to make mistakes.

One more word about timing: Erik might have been right; the apostrophe was in the wrong place. But pointing it out when and where he did was completely immaterial to our conversation about my department's strategy. That was like someone not signing an investment application for 7 million euros and blasting it back into corporate orbit because there was a spelling mistake. As a manager, you need to be aware that wherever your attention and energy go, the attention and energy of your organization follow. That's why the timing of discussions about mistakes is important as well. Take your time and find an attitude of "It would have been even better if..." instead of "You did something wrong." A document without typos, a graphic with correct captions, and a presentation without filler words: that's professional and that's where we want to be. As a manager, you should sense when energy is available for this and then make the appropriate room to place the joy of good results and a strong impact at the center of the conversation.

As a leader, each day you can promote courage and boldness, show trust, step aside, and see others grow – and thus grow yourself. Trust and courage are not one-way streets, but a source of higher impact, more joy in collaboration, and personal growth.

Leading People for More Courage

By asking questions that **invite courageous action**, you create the necessary space for new ideas, perspectives, and alternatives. You can encourage individuals by deliberately offering them a **risky task** that is seemingly "too big," in which they can experience and prove themselves. To get employees out of their comfort zone, managers can also **take a step back** from time to time – this is how courage grows. If you see someone who steps into the growth zone again and again – further **encourage and support them**. They can be a role model for everyone. In your leadership, make sure you strike a smart **balance** between recognizing and eradicating mistakes and giving energy to development opportunities, innovation, and new tasks.

Chapter 13

Courage to Change – Thinking Bigger

Transformation, innovation, change management, and many other terms (and attempts to implement them) are omnipresent in our work. The VUCA world and "normal" processes of change in our environment and in the organization repeatedly push us to the brink, where staying in the comfort zone is no longer an option. Here, we need courage, don't we?

When the House Is Burning

I started in market research at Procter & Gamble in the 90s. The department had a great reputation and a central place in decision-making processes. Regardless, the global head at the time launched a renewal process for the department. Fortunately, my manager sent me to the European working group, where I participated in the discussions first-hand. They began as they probably do thousands of times on such occasions. Well-established experts and successful managers discussed how they were doing everything right, pointing to success stories, the department's high reputation, and exciting projects. Until someone played devil's advocate. What if market research was outsourced and turned into an external service provider that had to compete against other such service providers with competitive offers? Such a wave of outsourcing was sweeping through specialist departments in many large companies at the time – so it was a real possibility, not simply a pipe dream.

This question shook us to the core. Were we really doing something that only we could do? How were our performance and contributions different from those of any market research institute or management consultancy?

Our discussions became much more heated. Suddenly, we were ready to question what we had achieved instead of idly patting ourselves on the back. That was the beginning of a comprehensive renewal of the market research department, and without someone acting as "the devil" the energy for it would not have been released.

This example is from early in my professional career, since then I have experienced situations like these dozens of times in organizations that

DOI: 10.4324/9781003582724-15

struggle to perceive and adapt to change. You are not alone if you are realizing that the "modus operandi" of your organization is no longer fit for the future. Digitalization spurts, the decarbonization of the economy, pandemic decrees, or unfamiliar expectations of young talent may disrupt your business model or your organization's reason for being. Take the opportunity to understand the root of the change, the risks and opportunities emerging, and put on the pressure – on yourself and your organization. Since things won't continue as they are, establish "the pull." The pull is the power, the will, and the curiosity to break new ground.

Courage for the Preservers

> I don't understand why people are afraid of new ideas. I'm afraid of the old ones.
>
> John Cage

Do you find it difficult to find the courage to innovate and make changes in your work? Do you enjoy your routines, the existing systems and find reasons not to participate in relevant working groups and projects? Do you maybe even ask yourself whether it might be courageous to preserve something and not follow every trend? Yes – it is courageous to formulate a different opinion and swim against the tide of those who believe in forever innovation. But it is also extremely unlikely that an organization that leaves everything as is will do so because that is truly the best way. It is much more likely, and I have observed this many times, that no one looks at how the world, people, and technologies are changing. The effects of these changes are played down, or only tentative adjustments are made (see Kodak, Nokia, Tupperware).

If you find change challenging, this may be due to personal preference. If you consistently adopt a defensive stance when it comes to innovation and change because you value your routines, what's familiar, and overrate risks arising – then that's how you are. This preference will not change thanks to pressure from superiors or the agitation of enthusiastic colleagues. If your personal preference is the familiar, the existing, and the routines, and you are challenged to change, try these steps:

1. Find out what the intention of the change is
2. Understand what new developments the changes are reacting to and what benefits they strive to create
3. Reflect on how exactly the upcoming changes are aligned with the new realities. Can the promised benefits be realized? How time-consuming, costly, and difficult will the change be?
4. What is your rejection about? Which of your needs are being hurt by the change? How does this affect you?

5 What can you do to correct or minimize the negative impact, and what to amplify potential good outcomes?
6 Only now should you draw a conclusion. Be as objective as possible and then find the courage to take the right next step
7 If you realize that you can understand the changes rationally but have a strong (negative) emotional reaction, then respect both! Your emotional reaction is most likely a "pain of parting" because the change affects your familiar social structure and that is difficult for you. Talk to others about this parting and see what you can carry into the future. Make plans that give you energy and optimism

These steps are not done in 10 minutes. They require as much curiosity, patience, conversations, and tolerance toward the "forever innovators" as understanding and attention toward yourself. Distinguish between facts, needs, and feelings but have respect for all three. Another piece of good news: after all the changes, your preference for routines and reliability will ultimately be satisfied again, and your courage to go along will have paid off. At the end of such processes, the new responsibilities, routines, and working methods have been agreed upon and learned, and everyone is happy that someone like you is applying them carefully and reliably.

Courage for the Rebels

You must have skipped the last chapter, so unfamiliar are you with the thought processes of the "preservers." Do their objections and concerns annoy you? Do you find them complacent, lazy, and unimaginative? Watch out. These people bring something precious to the party: they will ensure that important business practices continue and run smoothly, that you improve your persuasion skills, and that you find the weak points in your argumentation. And: these people are everywhere – just as there are rebels like you everywhere. We can wish each other away – or recognize and use each other's unique contributions.

Perhaps you feel just as alone in your joy of change as most others: Gallup, an international consulting firm, reported in 2018 from a representative survey of employees that 80% of respondents do not feel encouraged to try new things, fail, and learn from mistakes in their workplace. If you are working in such an environment and your ideas are constantly being rejected, then the courage crocodiles have already penetrated far into your working world. Such an organizational culture and working atmosphere cannot be changed by a single brilliant idea, a passionate speech at a management seminar, or a training session with an "innovation guru." It will take initiative, insistence, and patience. What can you do to create movement and openness for new things so that you and others can propose new ideas, approaches, and strategies?

1 Create as vivid a picture of your idea as possible, work out the advantages, and explain how it can work. Explain why "keeping it up" is wrong and a new approach is needed. Explain this over and over again – even if you can no longer hear yourself
2 Achieve early successes and make them known. By communicating and possibly even celebrating the achievement of agreed intermediate steps, you show everyone that the picture of success you are painting can become a reality
3 Find and mobilize allies, forge alliances with influential people in the organization. Don't discredit and humiliate your "opponents" and those more hesitant – you'll turn them away! Meet them with empathy, ask questions, and understand what is going on with them. Try to incorporate their objections into your ideas. Talk about common interests, complementary skills, and responsibilities, and create a "win-win" in which everyone involved sees and receives advantages
4 Respect the small steps and results and find a pragmatic attitude toward feasibility. For this book, I spoke to many people who have large ambitions for the sustainable transformation of our economy. Each of them recommended "pragmatism" in their work: even if no single step, no single project is sufficient to address the problem as a whole, it is only through these small building blocks that significant transformation is achieved
5 "Institutionalize the resistance" is a tip from Marion Sollbach, who for many years worked as "Head of Sustainability" at Galeria Kaufhof and Metro, among others. In corresponding working groups, reports in board committees, etc., skeptics and obstructionists must listen and justify their position. This is where you can obtain important information and opinions, present your concerns, explain yourself, and, if necessary, push through decisions. This is all part of the courage of change
6 There will be setbacks. Understand what went wrong. Learn from it. Improve and move on
7 Take note of the "tipping point," the moment when your project develops traction, you find real success, and you go from being the underdog to a leading figure. You now need a different kind of energy that radiates natural authority and no longer needs to nervously explain things. Ease, assuredness, and reliability are now expected of you, not rebelliousness
8 Don't triumph when you finally do succeed. The reluctant, hesitant, and cautious will suddenly want to be part of your success. Be generous, include them, and refrain from making any bitter remarks about the

exhausting or even hurtful past. Expand the concept of "The winner takes it all" to include your past opponents

Failure Is a Part of Life

Mistakes are a dread for many successful, high-performing, and ambitious people. We have already talked about this. Even worse when the overarching goal is not achieved: when they fail. However, failure is not the opposite of success, but part of it.

After starting my own company, I felt very much as if I was "failing" – between my picture of success and current reality was a canyon of unanswered contact requests, rejected offers, and webinars without registrations. Being self-employed includes that too. So, I analyzed the situation, took action (e.g., by writing this book), and tried (new) things out. It was really hard, and I persevered. This was part of my eventual success; I was absolutely convinced that my work was valuable and my contribution important. With this attitude, I developed new offers, revised my marketing strategy, and kept going – full of confidence that success will come. And it did.

Failure is the stressful side of courage. What defines risk is the possibility of "failure" – you don't achieve the goal you set out for, and it might cost you – energy, money, and a promotion. If you have an ambitious team, everyone is frustrated and disappointed when things go wrong. What you don't need in that moment is wasting energy on the blame game. Instead, mobilize your and the team's energy to get back to the purpose of your cooperation: "Why did we set this goal, and what do we do now that we haven't achieved it?"

Go into analysis to understand what you could do better in the future. Respect that not everything is controllable and manageable and that this time you didn't have that little bit of luck sometimes needed. Be proud that you tried something that was not easy to achieve. Now you can take responsibility for ensuring that your courage is not cataloged as a mistake but remembered as a lesson. This will depend on attitude, the questions asked, and the capacity to rethink the next steps and focus on the purpose of the endeavor (Table 13.1).

In failure, you will also discover whether your "purpose" is compelling. Whether "the pull" it creates is strong enough to continue. If everyone hits the sack after failing to achieve a goal, maybe it wasn't enough. There was too little conviction and passion to invest in analysis, in the next goal, or a follow-up plan after the initial frustration. Instead, accept the frustration, analyze the (root) causes, and move on smarter and with optimism. Good luck!

Table 13.1 Failure as a Teacher

Turning failure into a teacher

Posture	*Questions*	*Steps*
Empathic	How are we doing?	Grieving together, being frustrated, acknowledging the disappointment
Analytical	What happened?	"Merciless" discovery of the reasons for the outcome
Optimistic	What is our new intention? How do we serve our purpose in the future?	Setting a new goal, defining a fresh picture of success
Creative	What to change?	Defining how to move to a fresh picture of success

The Big Changes

Many organizations die because they didn't want to recognize external developments. With "*Get your ass up,*" you can encourage your team or your board to shine a spotlight on the blind spots, perceive weak signals early, and actively develop future scenarios. This can generate lots of courage for new projects, processes, and goals.

A transformation process can be very stressful for "preservers." *Asking questions*, seeking understanding, and looking for calmer waters in the future can make the process of change more bearable. Successful rebels *mobilize people and resources* for their ideas. They also invite the hesitant to join in and get on board, avoid polarization, and pave the way with pragmatic interim results.

In our VUCA world and with the resources and skills we currently have, we might fail with our goals and projects. Success is much more appealing. And that's why we try and why we may fail. *Failure is part of success, not its opposite.*

Chapter 14

Civil Courage

I would like to conclude this book with a call for civil courage. I have (hopefully!) given you strength for your personal courage in shaping your life as well as inspiration for professional courage in organizations and companies. Individual happiness and professional success are worth striving for – in a democratic society of personal freedom and mutual respect. On occasion, you may find yourselves in situations where fundamental rights or the safety of individuals are at risk. This calls for a special kind of courage – civil courage. When you take a risk because a value important to you has been violated, a person is in danger, or protecting our coexistence requires some kind of intervention. This is the courage with which you help a victim of a dangerous situation, intervene when people are insulted or humiliated in your presence, or when basic values of our coexistence are violated. Your civil, or moral, courage overcomes the fear of negative personal consequences and leads you to do the right thing.

> The more citizens with civil courage a country has, the fewer heroes it needs.
>
> Franca Magnani, cited in Böll (1987)

If you want to muster and strengthen your courage to prevent injustice or discrimination around you, look at your mindset, reflect, find allies, and start practicing. You can strengthen your mindset for civil courage by becoming conscious of your values: what is important to you in living and working together? When do others violate boundaries that you don't want to see violated? Who do you want to be in these circumstances, what do you want to stand for?

You can review the last four weeks, three months, six months, and see in which situations (your) lines were crossed. A sexist joke between colleagues? Someone being shamed for being less affluent? Racist remarks on the train? Remember how you felt in that situation and how you reacted, if at all. See what could have been a civically courageous interaction.

DOI: 10.4324/9781003582724-16

Mobilize allies by talking to people you trust, sharing your concerns about those situations and what you'd like to do in the future. Ask for their perspective and encouragement. Start practicing civil courage.

"It's never too late" – if the derogatory, abusive remarks are made repeatedly, among friends or in other social contexts, seek a conversation with the relevant person(s) away from the acute situation. It doesn't matter if you didn't dare to speak up the first time it happened. Talk about respectful and fair behavior. It will be even easier if you get together with a like-minded person and bring up the issue together. We cannot commission a respectful and just world. But in your life, there will be countless moments when you can decide to do your part.

Civil Courage

A democratic society of personal freedom and mutual respect needs commitment from every participant/member, and sometimes it also *needs their courage.*

You are "civically courageous" if you stand up for others who are dependent on someone's help because they are being threatened, discriminated against, humiliated, or cannot defend themselves (alone).

Just like individual courage, *civil courage is a skill.* Activate your moral compass, find options for action and possible allies to put an end to an intolerable situation.

Reference

Böll, H. (1987). *Feindbild und Frieden: Schriften und Reden 1982–1983. dtv Verlagsgesellschaft mbH & Co. KG.*

Chapter 15

Conclusion

About Me

Courage is individual and personal. In order to better understand my anecdotes and perspectives, I am happy to give insight into my values, how I see the world, and key moments in my life.

I am the youngest of six children. There was always someone there for me. To teach me, help me, or protect me. I am a person with a refugee and migrant background: my mother fled from Pomerania to Göttingen in 1945 at the age of 15. My father, a Frenchman, made a life for himself in Germany in the 1960s. For both my parents, curiosity about each other and their background was more important than the history of Franco-German enmity. I seem to have inherited this cultural and geographical mobility.

My father died far too young as one of the 20,000 annual traffic fatalities in the 1970s. The result was a life that perceives material wealth as something very fleeting and unreliable. Moral responsibility and social commitment shaped our upbringing and feel like the DNA of my German heritage. My half-aunt was executed by the Nazis in 1944 for "treason," a huge loss for the family, and her moral legacy was present in our upbringing. In my childhood, relatives from France, refugees from Chile, and young people in distress came to live in our spacious family home.

As described in the chapter on "Values," the values most important to me are "trust," "creativity," and "freedom."

I associate the value of trust with my great need to relate to other people, create something together, have friends, and experience wonderful things together. I love working with and in teams, being close to others, giving and receiving help. I am happy in my close family of five and part of a large and diverse extended family.

Upside

I rarely make promises I can't keep. I trust younger colleagues and they respond with high performance. I always look at the long-term impact of my actions.

DOI: 10.4324/9781003582724-17

Downside

I am very disturbed when I don't feel trust or when my trust is violated. Lies infuriate me and will quickly land me on the high horse of superior morality. Distrust hurts and unsettles me. I overwork myself to "earn" trust.

The value of "freedom" is important to me both physically and emotionally. Physically, the few times in my life when I didn't feel any freedom of movement – such as in North Korea, as a teenager at a sailing camp, or during some business trips in the evenings in a hotel – were unnerving. I couldn't really think of anything else but the ongoing curtailment of my personal freedom. The coronavirus lockdown, even though things went reasonably smoothly in Germany, was very stressful for me. In many life choices – e.g., how I deal with money or career moves – I pay attention to long-term freedom.

Upside

I can question a lot of things because I don't feel bound to certain answers and patterns. I am willing to challenge more powerful people because I see myself as independent of them.

Downside

Sometimes my need for freedom gets in the way of my "hunger for trust" – I have left companies out of curiosity and for independence. And then I sat somewhere new without my beloved colleagues.

Upside

Creativity is certainly another driver of my life. I instinctively look for new solutions, always asking myself "how can it be done faster, better, prettier." I paint, sew, and sing amateurishly – with a love of the experience and a sense of humor about the result. In everyday life, I like to live out my creativity by cooking. My ability to think "out of the box" is essential in all aspects of my life. In other words, I don't follow the conventional, established path, but ask whether there are completely different solutions. This is how I became a "thought leader" for my clients, a pioneer in strategically challenging topics. I can use my creativity to bring together a huge amount of data, information, and phenomena into a "story," which then provides clear orientation for management and marketing departments, for example. This is not a production of "alternative facts," but a special creative ability to discover the common thread, the pattern, the connecting factor in the jungle of data, and then to convey this to the audience in an exciting and possibly surprising way.

I have had many original, unique, and effective ideas and implemented them successfully. The creativity of others inspires me and always encourages me to find new ways myself. I have an exciting life that adheres little to convention and is driven a lot by curiosity.

Downside

I get bored of routine, even when it's the most efficient solution. It's a fine line between creativity and provisional solutions. I sometimes offend people for whom conventions are important.

Final Words

Courage is a skill, not a character trait. I very much hope that my book will empower you to cross the courage zone whenever it serves you well. Because it is beneficial in life not to resign yourself to circumstances, but to pursue your own wishes and to fulfill your needs. Many individual and collective opportunities arise when people act more courageously.

If you are looking for courage for your individual opportunities – with the five steps through the courage zone, you now know the way into the growth zone, where new skills, responsibilities, and life circumstances await. A courageous mindset will make it easier for you to recognize and overcome the(learned) fearmongers and courage crocodiles in the future. Intimidating, manipulative, and scary behavior loses its power when more people refuse to be brow-beaten and belittled. Too often, it is those with extended elbows, indifference, and egoism who take powerful positions. Recognize fear, cross your heart, understand reality, develop scenarios, find allies – and then courageously confront the fearmongers and perhaps reach for some power yourself.

Grasping for power – does that sound "evil"? Then replace "power" with "impact": reach for impact so that your environment, your team, and your company can create a courageous environment. This requires good foundations – purpose, goals, strategies, and clear agreements on working methods. And a courageous attitude with which we invite risk-taking and travel down new paths every day. I call for courage because we have huge tasks ahead of us. Fighting the climate catastrophe, living and doing business more fairly, and realizing human potential everywhere – we need a lot of courage for this, and it's not sitting in anyone's comfort zone.

With more courage in the world, we will experience more diversity, creativity, and joy. We will have better conversations, smarter solutions, and a more beautiful togetherness. With your courage, you will go through life with more impact, happily and fulfilled. That is my mission in writing this book: for you to discover and use new opportunities for your courageous action. Or to quote German football legend (and my childhood hero) Franz Beckenbauer: "Go out and play soccer!"

Index

Note: **Bold** page numbers refer to tables and *italic* page numbers refer to figures.

For Product Safety Concerns and Information please contact our EU representative GPSR@taylorandfrancis.com
Taylor & Francis Verlag GmbH, Kaufingerstraße 24, 80331 München, Germany

www.ingramcontent.com/pod-product-compliance
Ingram Content Group UK Ltd.
Pitfield, Milton Keynes, MK11 3LW, UK
UKHW020031260325
456732UK00014B/138
9781032949918